The Answer Is Energy

THE
Answer
IS
Energy

*A 30-Day Guide to Creating Your Ideal Life,
Embracing True Abundance,
and Knowing Your Worth From Within*

JARRAD HEWETT

NEW YORK

LONDON • NASHVILLE • MELBOURNE • VANCOUVER

THE *Answer* IS *Energy*

A 30-Day Guide to Creating Your Ideal Life, Embracing True Abundance, and Knowing Your Worth From Within

Published in New York, New York, by Morgan James Publishing. Morgan James is a trademark of Morgan James, LLC. www.MorganJamesPublishing.com

ISBN 9781642791587 paperback
ISBN 9781642791594 eBook
Library of Congress Control Number: 2018907524

Morgan James is a proud partner of Habitat for Humanity Peninsula and Greater Williamsburg. Partners in building since 2006.

Get involved today! Visit
MorganJamesPublishing.com/giving-back

TABLE OF
CONTENTS

PREFACE

As humans, we have this story that if something we perceive to be wrong happens, we immediately want to fix it. It's a natural impulse of the mind to fix and solve problems. So we try to fix the thing we see as broken, whether it be something within us, or in others. But what would happen, if instead of fixing or fighting, we allowed ourselves to be overcome with the love of pure spirit, pure source, and pure energy? What if we expanded our awareness beyond cause and effect, and into the realm of pure creation? I'll tell you: all of the spaces and places we thought we had to fix begin to fall away and change.

There's a space in our mind where we say, "No, no! This problem is so important! I need to really figure it out. I need to understand it." But what if you just let it go? Just let it go. What if you released the expectation of it ever coming back, so that there was no fear to disturb you? In a way, this process is like waking up. You've awakened to a new experience of your body and your life where you can allow yourself to be overcome by pure source energy. This is not about any person or place or even any set of rules. It is about your divine connection to all that is and all that will ever be.

When you fully allow that connection to ignite and blaze bright, there is nothing in the world that you cannot be or do. From this space, your whole being begins to change and align in new ways, with everything you've ever desired. Old tapes and physical issues you may have fought with for ten, twenty, or even thirty-plus years begin suddenly to dissolve.

Mastery is all about truly knowing love is all we need. However, in the physical body, we need food. We need shelter. We seek wellness and abundance, and the truth is, the gateway to this kingdom of receiving, is opening yourself up to Pure Love, and understanding that love is an energy which creates. As we journey into this space of knowing ourselves in a new way, we often run smack dab into old beliefs... the contrast we create to remind ourselves of what we truly desire.

This book is all about why we create that contrast and how we can let that go, so we may begin to truly live our passions and create our deepest desires.

On our thirty-day journey together, I am going to walk you through, step by step, just how energy creates through our thoughts, feelings, and beliefs, and show you how to shift into a paradigm of ease, bliss, love, abundance, and tranquility ... fast! And the best part about all of this is *it doesn't have to be hard.*

When I was a young child, I discovered I could see and hear things other people could not. I learned very quickly that was not something many folks in my conservative town were okay with. I was taught to hide who I was, because it was weird. It was wrong; I was wrong. As I grew, I manifested being morbidly obese by age 9. I had ulcers in third grade. I developed severe depression and anxiety in my formative years, because my inner world, who I really was, and my outer world, who I projected myself to be, were not in severe dis-harmony. As I shut my energetic heart down and closed off to the world, for fear of being known – and fear of knowing myself – my physical heart began to shut down. College was a series of emergency room visits and depressive episodes. My heart beat out of rhythm, and I did not see any space of freedom in sight.

Finally, one day, while lying in bed, I prayed for God to take me. I was tired of fighting. I was tired of being sick and feeling like I was nothing.

In that moment, a strange thing happened. I realized that as I let go of all of my stories of needing to fight and fix, I actually felt better; I felt free. It was in that moment that I realized that I had been living someone else's life. I had been filtering who I am through someone else's belief systems. I had always seen energy, yet I had refused to allow myself to open to this gift because I feared it. Yet, in opening up to myself, I truly began to see how everything in this life is energy.

I began to think, "Had I been born 3,000 miles away to a whole different family, with a different religion, different monetary background, and different family structure, would I still be who I am? How might I be different? Who am I beyond all of the thoughts and beliefs, and how have those thoughts and beliefs set in motion everything I have believed, wanted, and created – even sub consciously – my entire life?"

We are taught that we are the sum total of our past, yet the truth is, we don't even understand how that past has shaped and molded us, and that there is a space of divine love, greater than anything you may even be able to imagine right now, wherein you can change your entire trajectory in life.

You have the power to change who you are. You have the power to create whatever you desire.

Are you ready to learn how?

Ralph Waldo Emmerson once famously said, "Be not the slave

of your own past – plunge into the sublime seas, dive deep, and swim far, so you shall come back with new self-respect, with new power, and with an advanced experience that shall explain and overlook the old."

This book is the experience of a love so deep, you will not only be able to overlook and explain the old, you will be thankful for it. That may seem like a controversial statement, yet when you open to this new space of self-discovery, you find the magic was within you all along, and you are able to shine like never before.

How can you move from a space of fear into a space of creation – no matter what the subject? How does one learn to love, to forgive, and to create with no abandon?

The answer… is energy, and that answer is here. It is you. It is now. It is fun.

And it is easy.

INTRODUCTION

Often times, life can throw us curve balls. As we journey from adolescence into adulthood, we experience events, loss, and hurdles, which start to create this feeling of "I don't know if I can do this anymore. I don't know that I have it in me to create everything I desire in my life," be it in finance, relationships, career, health, or any other subject.

This feeling of not being or having enough creates a "squeeze" in our energy. We feel frustrated, angry, or we check out completely. We shut down, because we don't want to feel anymore. We start to loose connection to ourselves, to others, and even to the Divine, however we may define that.

We find ourselves a bit confused, lost, even.

Or maybe we have a fundamental understanding of what we want; we just can't seem to create it.

We are stuck in our relationships or our jobs. We take two steps forward, and then fall three steps back.

Why? Why do we experience these stumbling blocks in creation? Is it because we've done something wrong? Have we just not wanted it enough?

I pose to you the answer is actually much simpler: the answer is energy.

As we begin to dive into just what that means, and what the ramifications are, take a moment and feel into the following questions.

- What is the one thing in this world that you would like to experience more than anything else?
- What is the one thing you would like to create?
- What is the one thing you would like to release?
- If you could experience any miracle on this planet, what would it be?
- What would it be like to truly feel seen, and loved, nurtured and cherished?

Every answer you came up with is attached to a belief somewhere inside of you. It may be a belief about what you need in order to be happy or healthy, loved, or even simply a belief about what "doing better" means to you, based on stories you've been told, and stories you now tell yourself. We have beliefs about what feelings are allowed and not allowed, how we are supposed to act and express, and what we are even capable of, in the first place.

Even as adults, when we tell ourselves we should know better, we carry our wounds, and they become our dominant thoughts. They become lodged in our physical bodies, in our thoughts patterns, our emotions, and they begin to form the song of our being. But when we begin to let go of some of those old tapes, we can spark the flames of transmutation so the old wounds can finally heal, and a new creation can be birthed.

There's an old analogy about building your castle on sand. Many of us whether it is emotionally, physically, mentally, or spiritually have built our castles on sand. We've built on foundations that at the time seemed solid enough to give us a start, but as we've progressed as people and as we've progressed as consciousness, our foundation began washing away. We start to panic thinking, "I'm losing everything. I'm losing it all." But there is a space and place where who you really are, beyond your stories, is simply asking you to let go of the limitation you've placed on who you are and how you create.

Change doesn't have to mean everything is crashing down on top of you. Change is there to help you grow and thrive. It's just the vibrational equivalent of snapping your fingers and finding yourself in a space that's ever changing. And you are fluid enough to change with it! You just don't always know it.

When the winds of change begin to stir our soul, we set out on a journey in the search for answers. We would love the Red Barron to fly by and skywrite in the sky, "Hey! This is what you're supposed to do!", but it's never that easy. Sometimes we feel jolted, inspired, or simply bereft of ideas and left with no option but to embrace change.

We all feel it in different ways, but whatever it is, are you ready to let it be easy? Are you ready to know yourself and love yourself in a whole and new way?

In this book, I'll take you on a thirty-day journey and teach you how to tap into actual energy and easily create a space to release your blocks around all areas of life: money, love, relationships, fear, pain, grief, family, and many more.

I wrote this book so that you can learn who you are, outside of your stories. I wrote it to help you have a greater understanding of the world, the Universe, and yourself and to experience life fully as you release and free yourself from all doubt, blame, guilt, shame, old stories and worn out belief systems, and the judgment of others.

With this book, I promise you will find the inspiration to make changes that will guide your energetic frequencies in the direction of love, abundance, peace and freedom.

There is that space where we want to wait to make a shift in our lives. We want to get everything perfect before we step out, take a risk, and just leap. It's like checking that parachute eighteen million times before you jump out of a plane. Well, sometimes, we get so caught up in checking the parachute, our plane lands and we realize we forgot to jump. We missed the adventure. In the midst of our checking and re-checking, we may have even forgotten that we wanted to have an adventure in the first place.

Don't let yourself miss out on what you truly desire.

Trust yourself.

You can't get it wrong.

You *won't* get it wrong, as we journey into wholeness, freedom, joy, and light.

Welcome to your new Self.

This is the first page of a whole new book, written just for you.

To download your free meditation starter kit,
visit www.jarradhewett.com/meditations. Enjoy!

CHAPTER 1

WHAT IS ENERGY?

I am asked this question repeatedly.

"What is energy work? Is it some esoteric, out there, woo-woo concept?"

The simple answer is, "Yes. It is." But energy work is based on much more than just a mere theory or idea. It's rooted in science.

I remember my grade school class looking at cells and atoms through a microscope. Even though I believed trees or concrete were solid, I could see through a high-powered microscope and see through solid objects. We were viewing a collection of cells, atoms, and neutrons- everything coming together in proportion to the amount of positive and negative charges, the density, or the amount of light they were able to hold or carry that gave them their density. It was the density that gave them their physical vibration so that energy became a solid mass.

And that's what you are. You are energy in all its various forms.

Every single thing in this Universe has energy – the feeling, the emotion, the tangential experience of joy and love. All of these have an energetic frequency. You may think about knowing yourself in the context of your ego – as separate, as an individuation. While you *are* an individual, you are much more significant.

You are an individual expression of the light.

I got used to being in the emergency room a lot as a teenager and having to struggle with my own body- feeling comfortable and feeling safe. I was calling on an energy that would help shift my frequency from one of fear and anxiety to one of relief and security. My experience is such a metaphor for understanding that we are how we live in this world, and our relationship to God or Source. However you describe it, it's the creative force that is behind everything. When you tap into the unified field of everything – the "space beyond the space"- whether you call it God, whether you call it Creation, whether you call it Source – whatever that energy is, it is a tangible, readable energy.

If you've stood next to someone on a subway, you know that people give off heat. Maybe you stepped into a mall at Christmas time, or a crowded shop and you've felt that frenetic wave of energy. You might turn on a news program with guests arguing over hot-button issues. You feel your face suddenly getting warmer and your blood pressure rising. Those are physical signs of you absorbing that energy. You can feel it all over your body. You begin to tune into the frequency being broadcast at the time; honing into the emotional frequency of the overall event.

Think about frequency like a radio station, a spectrum on the AM or FM dials. You can turn it to 99.5, and you may hear a sad country song. You can turn it over to 102.7, and you may listen to an upbeat song that makes you want to dance. Your energy field is the same thing. Within your energy body, every thought, feeling, or emotion you experience has a different frequency, and every single one of those sensations registers energetically.

Every person on the planet has an electromagnetic field. When you go into the hospital for an EEG or an EKG, they put little nodes all over your body. The nodes transmit the energy you're sending, and the doctor receives a readout of your frequency. The doctor can also attach the nodes to your head to monitor the signals from your brain, which is emitting an active, energetic signal at all times. Whether it's tickling, pricking your toe with a needle, reading your favorite childhood book, or a sense memory or smell, the frequency your body is sending out will change according to the stimuli introduced to your body.

Energy work is introducing a different frequency into your field. We're taking the radio dial of our entire being and changing not just one or two stations on that FM dial, but considering the being-ness of all the facets of who you are. We're considering your relationship to money, career, interpersonal relationships, familial relationships, and romantic relationships, your health and illness – and transforming them into implements of love.

Energy and frequency are one. You're turning the dial, redirecting your energy mindfully and consciously creating where you want those frequencies to be. You're realigning places within your body so the output, your symphony, will sound the best it can sound. Your relationships are more joyful and fulfilling. Your experience with money is abundant and less complicated. Your experiences with love, with your body, your experience with health all begin to change by rehearsing your orchestra and fine-tuning the frequency you're broadcasting.

Energy powers every incandescent bulb, candle, sparkler, lightning bug and twinkle light. It is your source of power to illuminate the world and broadcast your beautiful symphony for all to hear.

You are the light.
You are the music.
You are the energy.

MEDITATION

My body is filled with buoyant joy and possibility.

My capacity for abundance, joy, and fulfillment is endless.

With every breath I take, I inhale peace and exhale love.

I AM love at its deepest level. I AM one with the energy which powers the stars.

I AM perfect just as I am.

I AM loved by all that is.

CHAPTER 2

THE MOMENT OF NOW

"My Partner wants a commitment,
but I'm not ready."

"I need to make more money if I want to be
financially solvent."

"The current political climate is wreaking
havoc on my nerves."

"Will I ever be able to thrive in a world where
everything feels so desperate?"

There are times in life when you feel like the world is pushing you into a corner. You gradually begin to feel a mounting source of pressure around you – in your relationships, finances, political discussions and conversations around current events. You sense that life is starting to intrude: as if you've nabbed a seat all to yourself on the bus and a man with three pieces of wheeled luggage plops down beside you, your little vestige of peace now rudely infringed upon. You begin to feel the baggage of the world pressing against you, straining at the seams, ready to burst at the zippers.

The pressure is starting to take up precious real estate in your outer energy fields and is now flooding into your energy body. You think, "How did this happen, and WHY is it happening to ME?" while you squirm – compressed, caged, and terribly uncomfortable. Slowly, anxious thoughts and feelings seep into all your spaces and places, muscling their way into your internal speak and leaving you feeling as though you have no room to breathe within your own body. When the anxiety hits critical mass and you've been barricaded into a corner, your emotions sizzle like a lit stick of dynamite ready to blow. What began as a small flurry of stress has now snowballed into an avalanche of angst and at that moment you do what you feel is your only option.

You begin to push back.

Resistance is the cement that creates the prison of pressure, worry, and fear in your energy field. In a metaphysical way, resistance not only builds and re-enforces the fortress, it invites *more* struggle in. According to the law of attraction, if you're yelling, "No, no, no, no, NO!" resistance cannot hear you. But with laser precision, it homes in on your vibration, and your vibration is screaming, "UGHHH!"

The Universe was keenly aware of the signal you sent out. It picked up your energy loud and clear. It replied politely, "We heard your request, and as a courtesy, we'd like to present you with a heaping helping of "UGHHH" on the house. It was a pleasure to serve you. You're welcome!" In bellowing out the "UGHHH" energy, you transmitted a powerful call to action. The cage you were pressured into did not suddenly appear from nowhere. You requested it.

But here's a thought. What if you needed no boundaries because your presence spoke for itself? What if you needed no boundaries because your presence alone would be the sacred space where you have joy for no reason – the space where you do not need permission to do anything – the space where you were liberated and free?

So often we go back to our inner child that needs our mother's or father's permission that needs the Universe or God – we find ourselves seeking the permission to be successful, seeking validation to be worthy, seeking justification to know your own worth, know your own goals, and know our own value out in the Universe.

But what if you didn't need permission to do anything? What if you had value intrinsically inside you, (which you absolutely do) What if you remembered that every day?

What if your presence sparked its own awareness?

What would you be like?

Who would you be like?

What are the attributes that you describe for yourself?

Where you've been has brought you to where you are. No boundaries, no pushing, no paralysis.

Where you are is in the moment of NOW.

Had you not been where you were, things may have been very different. But you're here and you're here right now. In the moment of now is where you have the power to transform. You have the power to change anything and everything. If you can just accept that you are right now *right now,* you can accept yourself fully. In the present you can unlock a beautiful power. You can unlock that presence – a presence that speaks for itself. Boundaries are no longer needed because your powerful, loving, all-encompassing presence is so strong.

What if there was no judgment or pressure in your energy field? What if it was a space of no comparison and no compromise? What if there was a space where you didn't compare yourself to anyone else – not your siblings, your spouse, your parents, neighbors, coworkers? Not even the alternate version of yourself that we sometimes create within ourselves? You know that version of you very well. It's the "I should have" version of ourselves or the "what if" version of ourselves that says, 'Well, had I done these things differently, this is who I would have been and I would have preferred to be *that* person – not who I am today.'

As you start on your spiritual journey you may think, "Well, I should be 'this' by now." What if you could just let that go and allow yourself a place of no judgment? Just too really feel the freedom – the freedom to feel what is right now? What if you allowed that light from within to shine so bright that you began to see that there is possibility everywhere? That there is joy to be had everywhere? A place where you could go out and have fun, no matter what? What if the fear and resistance began to lift off and you could feel into that beautiful sense of awe and joy that knows no pressure, no angst, or no intrusion – a freedom that comes with open sky, open hearts, and boundless love?

What if you lived solely in the moment of now?

MEDITATION

I know that the past is the past.

I forgive myself and all others for any interactions or creations I may have knowingly or unknowingly been dragging into my present.

I choose to be born again, right now, in a new space and energy of Divine Love, freeing me to unwrap the present of all I am, unfolding in love, in the moment of now.

I release myself from any "should" energy, allowing my future to be a blank canvas, created through and by love, as the choices I make right now, starting with the choice to love myself, and all I AM.

———————————————————————

CHAPTER 3

THE SHIFT

I f you asked me to describe my youth, there are a few words that come to mind.

Trapped. Scared, Afraid: basically miserable.

I was miserable for the first two decades of my life. I lived in a state of deep sadness and confusion. I didn't understand why I was put on this earth. If you had told me I had *chosen* to be here, that concept would have been entirely foreign to me. I would have had no idea what you were talking about. My thought would be, "How could anyone choose to come into such an awful place where people are cruel, uncaring, controlling, selfish and greedy? Why live in a world where the system is the way it is?" I had a very "outside in" view of the world as opposed to "inside out."

Much of the confusion I experienced in my youth stemmed from the gift that I was born with. As a little boy, I could see and hear the energy of those around me. But, because of the way I was brought up, I wasn't supposed to feel the intense vibration that was flowing through me. At a very early age, I got the message that I was different.

Not everyone is in a space where they recall being born with these gifts. However, there's a universal template that many of us fall into in this world. We are taught, in some way shape or form, to diminish who we are. We are encouraged to hide our light. We are told that who we are is not okay and often, through trauma, a wound, or abuse energy, we begin to feel like an outsider.

I too began to shut myself down, shut myself off, and withdraw from life and the world. The only way I knew how to process energy and feelings was to eat them, to stuff them in my mouth and swallow them. Overeating, especially at an early age when my habit developed, was a way to process the energy and per-plexity I was experiencing. I didn't know how to integrate my emotions or surroundings, so my way to cope was to embrace food. After gobbling down my pain and uncertainty, my body then stored them as fat.

By age nine, I was close to 200 lbs. – morbidly obese and abso-lutely miserable.

As I grew older, I continually got the message that I "didn't fit in," "wasn't good enough," and "wasn't worthy." Who I was as a person, the abilities and talents bestowed on me – even the genu-ine soul I possessed underneath was branded as "wrong." I didn't understand at the time what my incredible gift *was*. I thought it was very much a curse. So I accepted my fate.

"I am broken."

But I wasn't broken. I wasn't wrong. I wasn't unworthy.

I was an empath.

I could feel other people's pain. In fact, *all* I could feel was the pain. I didn't realize I could switch a channel within myself to feel the joy and the love inside me. So all I felt every day was sorrow and pain – my own and that of the others around me. I know some of you may identify strongly with those feelings and experiences.

I was told continuously through the messages of religion and the misunderstandings of the people around me that I was "not right." My family members had their own stories and were projecting those stories onto me. They didn't mean to create those feelings in me, and they did not have ill wishes. They were trying to protect me and do what they thought was best for me. They were trying to "save my soul" by keeping me away from these things because they didn't understand that these were innate gifts I possessed.

As my body comprehended all this, the "I am broken" energy intensified within me. It started to process in my heart, and that began to shut my heart down through rhythm disturbances and valve problems. I was not able to stay in rhythm with my own body and unable to sync my own heart. My heart was home, and my home was broken. I was literally walking to the beat of a different drummer. I hit a tipping point where I knew I had to take stock of my life and examine not what others thought of me, but what I thought of myself.

"What do I believe about myself?

"I believe I'm broken."

Check.

"I believe I'm not supposed to feel the way I feel."

Check.

"I'm not supposed to do the things I do."

Check.

"I'm wrong in this way, this way, this way, and this way."

Check. Check. Check. Check.

I had it all figured out. I ticked off all the boxes. Broken and wrong. Done and done. Case closed.

But somewhere deep in my heart, I knew the labels that had been plastered on me since childhood weren't correct. I recognized that the stories other people had foisted on me were not mine. A revelation was brewing, and then it hit me. The question wasn't *what* I believed about myself. The problem was, "*Why* do I believe it?" The answer came quickly.

"I believed it because someone else told me to."

I started to realize where I was living someone else's belief systems. As I felt into that, I began to respond physically. I would have moments where my heart would beat rapidly, or it would beat back in sync. I noticed the physiological response that correlated with the thoughts I was thinking. I became acutely aware when my body felt better. I noticed my anxiety subsiding. The crippling depression was suddenly lifting. It was literally like a miracle. It was like an enormous, gray cloud dissipated and revealed a shining sunbeam.

My first thought was, "What just happened?" And I began to process it put the pieces together step by step.

This was a belief I held about myself that just lifted out.

What was this belief?

Was it a core belief that I'm not supposed to be here in my power, and I don't belong?

Yes and that belief didn't come from me. It came from someone else.

I recognized it, I let it go, and now I am here in my power. I'm plugging into all the times when other people abused their power, and I'm feeling the guilt and the shame of what power has brought in some other cases in life. I realized that was something I learned from others.

These beliefs were never mine, and I'm ready to let that all go.

There it was. I had shifted my energy from *broken and wrong* to *powerful and free*.

It was then that I began to look at all of life as a system of energy. I looked at everything as energy- not just the mental constructs, but my physical body as well. Whether it's a tree, our solar system, our emotions or our thoughts. It's all held together in a unified field of energy.

There were days in my teens where I looked at a bottle of pills and opened the top, took a pill, and thought, "I don't ever want to wake up." But I'm glad I did wake up. I was too young to realize that I had the power within. I wasn't ready to accept that power at the time. I was firmly planted in the space of giving up. But the same energy that creates within us the desire to give up can be harnessed and shifted. The energy source that fuels the overwhelming feeling or thought that says, "I've had it. I want to give up. I can't do this anymore." is the same beautiful energy source that empowers us to change that belief radically. We always have the power to redirect the energy – channeling its frequency out of the darkness and into the light.

Right now can be a brand new moment of birth – that every second you've lived until now can be a past life that we can transmute and release, so you can be born again. Everything you want to change can change. Everything you want to grow into can take shape and emerge, not just in your energy field, but also in your physical reality, so it can manifest instantaneously in your life.

Just like the enormous gray cloud that lifted for me, everything you've wanted to fall away can lift off so source energy can shine – illuminating your magnificent life.

MEDITATION

In this moment, I am opening up to see my life as Choice and Light. I know that I may have made decisions in the past which created disharmony for me and I am acknowledging that I am now ready to create harmony through loving myself and being responsible for my own vibrations. I know that my capacity for abundance, joy, and fulfillment is endless.

I AM love at its deepest level.

I AM perfect just as I AM, always expanding, always learning, and always loved by All That Is.

Right now, in this moment, I choose to believe that. I choose to feel that. I make this my truth.

CHAPTER 4

CREATING WORTHINESS

As a kid growing up very overweight, sickly, and always breaking bones, entertainment was my great escape. I had always been interested in TV, film, and cartoons. There was something so inviting about that magical landscape. So when I was ready, still thinking I was dying, of course, I decided that entertainment was it. Before I gave up the ghost and succumbed to my awful and tragic life, I wanted to move to Los Angeles.

When I moved to Los Angeles, I had just gotten up the energy to say, "OK, I may kick the bucket in the next year. I've got that much time."

It was time to decide.

"What *do* I REALLY want to do with my life?"

I managed to score a great internship working in entertainment. Part of my new narrative became, "I'm so excited that I'm healthy enough and feeling good enough to explore the world and enjoy my body in ways that I feel supported." Although sunshine and palm trees now surrounded me, I was still clinically diagnosed with agoraphobia and anxieties, so just leaving the house made my heart rate shoot up to 200. It was incredibly challenging, and it scared the ever-loving crap out of me.

But looking back and knowing what I know now, as an empath, I was feeling the energy of everyone around me and not understanding the energetic gift I embodied. The world was a much scarier place. I was bombarded by things I didn't know how to process. I decided to turn my confusion into a positive.

While in LA, I had begun dabbling in small energy workshops on my own. My friend Dee Wallace and I were working on a project together and she asked me to help facilitate a larger workshop with her. It was there that Dee taught the group the "I'm So Excited" exercise. The objective is to state something big or small that would make you feel supremely excited like, "I'm so excited I won the lottery!" or "I'm so excited I went to that big job interview!"

When it was my turn to tell the world with great glee what I was so excited about I yelled, "I'm so excited my body is supporting me on this journey! I'm so excited that I'm finally feeling good!" So that you know, I felt like a TOTAL idiot when I made these statements. So did the people who spouted their joy over hypothetically winning the lottery or landing a fictitious job interview. We all felt pretty ridiculous at first. But the more we ramped up our enthusiasm and just let ourselves play with the idea of something wonderful beyond measure, our joy grew. In fact, it grew exponentially. When we ramped up our energy and had fun with the process of possibility we began making breakthroughs.

At the time of the workshop, I was fairly new to my voiceover career. While I had landed past gigs for regional commercials, I hadn't booked a really HUGE national campaign yet. This was my opportunity to acknowledge that I desired something even bigger. I said, "I'm so excited that I'm able to lend my voice to something fun!"

This small declaration was an enormous step for me at the time. Just by saying the words made me feel victorious.

As time passed I remembered how empowered I felt doing the "I'm So Excited" exercise. I decided to set my sights on bigger aspirations. I thought to myself, "What's the biggest brand name in the United States? Coca-Cola! Wouldn't it be awesome if I landed an account like Coca-Cola?" I unleashed my inner ambition and let it all out, "I'm so excited that I'm the voice of Coca-Cola!"

Cut to the a few months later. The Fox Network's hit TV show American Idol was airing during the 2010 Winter Olympics. Television viewers all over the country were tuning in to watch the most recognizable sporting event, the most recognizable smash TV program on the air and featuring commercials from Coca-Cola, one of the world's most recognizable brands.

The voice of the Coca-Cola national ad campaign – the one millions of people heard at every commercial break during two blockbuster TV events, the one that just wanted to participate in "something fun?"

That "voice" was my voice.

Landing the Coca-Cola contract was an absolute dream come true. When I heard the news that I'd gotten the job, just as I did in that workshop, I yelled, "I'M SO EXCITED THAT I'M THE VOICE OF A NATIONAL CAMPAIGN FOR COCA COLA!!!"

It was real. And I was so excited.

When I first did the exercise, I started jumping up and down, and I'm sure I looked like a weirdo, but that's the space to celebrate that magical childlike wonder. Your happiness frees up those spaces and places we bury deep within our own body. You can do years' worth of energy work in an instant- grabbing that one precious moment of allowing yourself to blast your heart wide open to the joy, excitement, and the awe-inspiring fun that comes from letting your guard down and celebrating your blessed, soulful creation. It's a shame we don't let ourselves revel in euphoric vibration daily. It's a sin we don't permit ourselves to tune into the joy we created and take pride in the incredible accomplishments that are inherently ours and don't allow ourselves to celebrate from our hearts the jubilant beings we truly are.

In the wake of a job well done, people around you may jovially pat you on the back and say, "That's SO GREAT! Congratulations!" You, uncomfortable with the attention, smile and sheepishly reply, "Oh, thanks. That was fun." or mumble another self-deprecating response that minimizes your greatness. Deep down you feel the twinge of heaviness in your throat chakra or the mounting doom that deftly whispers in your ear.

"You're big time now, but watch out. Someone will take it all away from you."

"Don't draw too much attention; you'll look like a braggart."

Those toxic messages hang heavy in the air whether they're spoken or unspoken. You try not to listen, but those tireless voices just won't quit.

"Hey kid, don't get too big and forget us."

"You'll never do it again."

"Oh, look at you! You think you're better than us!"

Here's something you need to know, these words do not belong to you. They're not yours to carry. They do not show up in the narrative of your brilliant life. This is the time to rejoice in something wonderful. To rejoice in *your* wonderful. This is the space of saying, "No. I accept it because I AM it. I'm celebrating the heck out of all this because it's fun. I'm fun! I'm here to do it all. I'm here to create many masterpieces. That's what I want."

I can't tell you the amount of bravery it took to admit to myself, (and it sounds silly now), that as someone who had never booked anything even on a local level – I wanted a national, monstrously huge brand campaign. It took what felt like big cajones for me to write that down as my statement for myself and use it as the inspiration for the "I'm So Excited" exercise. I allowed myself to embrace that exercise with all my heart, and as a result, in a matter of weeks I had booked the national brand campaign I longed for. Those Coke spots were broadcast on televisions all over the world. I am living proof that whatever you want to create, you can create. No matter who you are or where you come from, you are worthy of your vision, expression, and the wildest creative dream come true.

You may try the "I'm So Excited" exercise, and think immediately, "I can't do it. I didn't do it right. I'm failing at it." That's you repressing your inner child. It's the horror of taking a risk. It's the fear of leaping into the unknown.

The mystifying, wondrous, abundant unknown.

MEDITATION

Here's the thing.

You've done the work.

There are no blocks.

You're on the plane.

You have your parachute on.

You've checked it 5000 times.

The parachute works.

We're up here.

We're at altitude.

It's time to jump.

It's your turn to say,

"Am I going to jump?"

"Do I truly want to create what I want to create?"

"Am I willing to run toward that beautiful yet terrifying vibration?"

Let your answer be yes because, believe me; it will change your life in ways you can't imagine.

So right now, make a list of three things you'd like to experience, and then start to get crazy excited as if they were here right now! That allows your vibration to move into a state where like attracts like.

The universe says, "Oh my goodness, look at that! The resonance is changing so fast, we better start creating and moving to align."

Grant yourself the joy of true play and celebration, and let the universe come into alignment to bring you even more.

CHAPTER 5

OUR STORIES

You may have heard the biblical quote, "It's easier for a camel to pass through the eye of a needle than a rich man to enter the kingdom of Heaven." In olden days, the "Eye of the Needle" was not actually a metaphor, but a narrow gateway into Jerusalem, and because camels were so heavily loaded with goods, they would need to unload everything they carried in order to pass through. The idea of the rich man moving through the eye of that needle isn't a knock on money, or even a reproach on wealth. It's actually a straight forward narrative about who we think we are and why we sometimes find it hard to shift into new ways of thinking or being, and why we sometimes find ourselves stuck in life. Here, the "rich man" simply has a lot of stuff he doesn't want to let go of, because it defines who he is. The baggage he carries represents his wealth, accomplishments, stories, and ultimately, his identity. And, in order to go through the gates, he has to be willing to put down all of the things he thinks make him who he is, and let go. He has to be willing to let go of all of the things he thinks make him who he is, because those very same things are what make it impossible to create something new.

That's the mind construct of the identity. We are not our jobs, our belongings, or our "stuff." Who we really are is the release of all that identity. It's not just "rich men" who can't enter the kingdom. It's the person who's still holding on to heartbreak 20 years after their divorce who can't get in. The person who still feels unworthy can't enter because they carry so much baggage around about who they are and what they can allow.

Whether we know it or not, in many ways, our minds work like computers, picking up little things here or there:

Learning at a young age to "sit down and be quiet," yet wondering why we can't quite speak up for ourselves at work all these years later.

Sometimes, we learn that it's not proper to ask for what we want, or we're simply not supposed to be powerful people. We aren't supposed to create. That's God's job – and who are you to think you are God?

The collective has years and years of repression and suppression around power, which often manifests in little hidden belief systems, running like a conflicting program in the back of our minds and energy fields, saying:

"I'm not allowed in my power. I don't belong."

We all have our inner belief systems, often in layers: whether they are genetic beliefs that have been passed down from our parents or grandparents, through the family of humankind, through different religious beliefs, or something we may have even noticed in other people and decided, "Hey, I think I'm gonna try that one!" Often times, they aren't even beliefs that we think would consciously support us in our creation. For example, sometimes, we see other people suffering, and rather than rock the boat, or invalidate their suffering by celebrating who we are, we lower our own inner light, and create a belief "it's not okay to shine. Others suffer so must I."

Many times, we also subconsciously take on someone else's suffering or poverty consciousness, believing if we can heal it within ourselves, we can someone help heal it within them; we can jump into the mud with them and somehow help lift them out! Unfortunately what that does is create a whole new template of suffering in our lives and we lose sight of our own existing goals. Now, we're not only dealing with our own stuff, but we're taking on new baggage that's weighing us down.

When we say, "don't belong in my power" that means, "When I get the power (abundance, love, etc. which makes me feel like a powerful creator), I have to bring in something to challenge or take away that power – something to knock me back a few steps, so I can validate: "See? Who do you think you are? You don't belong in your power." The thing we bring in is "limitation" and we often experience this in the form of what we dub as "other."

Someone or something else is doing this.

What "other" does is, it allows us to say "I don't create my own life. Other people, other circumstances, other things outside of me create my life." So as we empower ourselves, we bring in *other* to challenge our empowerment and instead of seeing that as an opportunity to say, "I'm going to end this abuse. I'm going to stand up and *shine* my light. I'm going to allow myself to be the light and hold the light and experience the light that I am." Instead, we respond with, "There's this giant thing outside myself. It's coming right at me like a giant wave that's about to consume me. It's taking all of my energy just to resist it. I'd better start to dim my light, and I'd better get in line, and I need to go back to suffering because that's better than the obliteration that's about to occur if I step into my full power."

There's a wonderful place where when you see a beautiful sunset, or you see a child or an animal; you have that moment of connection. Sometimes that moment of connection is so deep, that it will bring up tears. We don't necessarily have a conscious reason why we're crying; there's just a visceral connection that sparks deep emotion. Sometimes, when we feel connected, we cry. We cry because we feel the Oneness. In our daily lives, we're striving for that unity because we feel disconnected. Whatever the energy we've taken on, we feel separated. We yearn for unity conscious. We long for connection and being oneness. We crave nurturance and acceptance. When we connect with that moment, and our tears and emotions begin to flow, what we are tuning into at an often times unconscious level, is appreciation and Unity. It's such a huge space that we become overwhelmed. Our hearts swell with appreciation and love.

That space can also expose within us the gap where we're not living in that appreciation and love one hundred percent of the time. It is possible to live there and we tell ourselves it's not necessarily easy when there are people in our life who don't understand or recognize the importance. The truth is we don't always recognize the importance.

To live a life of full authenticity, let yourself off the hook a little. As best you can, choose to release yourself from any cords or contracts – any place where you've given your power away somebody else, any space where you've let attachment to being right take away focus on creating happiness, or any space where you aren't allowing yourself to be 100 per cent honest about your feelings.

Know that when limitation knocks on your door, and you let in the old stories of unworthiness, you're really just choosing to listen to the old recordings of whom you should be, or who you thought you were ... up until this new moment.

Within you, (beyond the stories, the collected memories of who you are, and the collected experiences you've had), the total of all that you are, is divine love. A lot of people have stories around "divine love": what they have to do to earn it, what they have to do to get it, and what they have to do to keep it. But none of that matters. When you fully embrace that you *are* divine love, you can unwind. You're free to unravel all the stories of who you think you are and who you have become. It allows you to begin to experience from within in that space, that you are. You are the connection, the love, the appreciation and the joy. As you begin to change your inner reality, the outer reality begins to mirror the inner reality.

One of the easiest things to do when you begin to change your inner reality is to *feel*. Feelings often bring up some stuff in our bodies and our cellular memories, because we have certain rec- ollections and templates and programs on how we're supposed to feel. But many times, when we go into a feeling, what we're actu- ally feeling is a thought.

What feels good? Let me think about it and then feel the thought.

But, what does a feeling feel like, free from story?

When we feel into a thought, often times, we are feeling a lim- itation or something in our mental body. And, in this moment, you are more than able to open up to feeling your feelings straight from the heart – separate from the mental body, separate from your stories. You can allow yourself permission to feel worthy. Allow yourself to feel love and connection. Your mind may say, "But to be worthy I have to do *this* or *that*." Picture in your mind an electronic button. When you press that button, you stop that thought. That thought is not bad. That thought is not something "separate" or "out to get you." It's just there. It's based on things you've experienced in the past. In a way, it's there to protect you because you've built up all these mechanisms that say, "Okay, I need to stay out of my power. Let me build this gigantic system to signal myself when I get too close." But you can bypass the mental bodies and the mental feeling places where you're feeling thoughts and open up to feeling your heart, feeling the love of *Source*, to feeling the support and empowerment. Even if this is something you've never experienced or never had the thought you could experience, allow the energy to move out feel to what it would feel like to live in a peaceful, loving universe. Not the definition of "peaceful" but *actual peace*. Just let the tranquility, calmness, and stillness wash over you. You're not bringing in any stories of what others would have to do, of what you would have to do, but knowing that beyond that, beneath that, unraveled at the core of that, beyond the story there is peace.

The time has come to open yourself up to experiencing wholeness and compassion, love of self and others that remain constant throughout our lives. This is not an exercise where you'll say, "I felt great for an hour, and then it all came back." It's about you putting your stories and baggage down and going through the eye of the needle. Like the rich man, you have to drop all your stuff to move into the true open heart, the ascended heart, and the kingdom – the place where everything is created. That is the space and place where you've not only lost all the stories; you've lost all the attachment to needing those stories or validating those stories. You've moved into a space where you can purely live, be, and breathe in the heart space.

MEDITATION

Who would I be if I let go of all my stories?

What stories am I not yet ready to give up?

Why won't I let them go?

Right now, I choose to let go of needing to know why or how. I choose to allow myself to feel good in this moment, because I am a beautiful creation of Love.

I release my past, and I choose feel what it feels like to truly know I am the energy of joy and bliss.

I now know that I don't need a complex problem to prove my worth, define myself, or earn love. Because I am Love.

CHAPTER 6

WHO AM I?

If you had met me about twenty years ago, you wouldn't have recognized me. I had clinical anxiety, clinical depression and PTSD. I was terrified to leave my own house. At one point, I had traveled outside the city for a weekend getaway to join some friends at a cabin. When the weekend was over, I was so afraid to get in the car and drive back to my house that I ended up staying in the cabin for six weeks. I literally couldn't leave. That's how afraid I was to be out in the world.

I was diagnosed with agoraphobia, the Greek term for "afraid of the marketplace." For me, it was essentially a fear of people, places, and things. It was later discovered that events I experienced as a child and a young adult spurred this intense anxiety. Home, and indeed, my experience of the entire world, was "wrong."

From a very early age, I could see energy, but I was born into a very strict conservative household which told me that my gift was a curse. It was wrong. It was a very fear-based understanding, but as a young man, I felt I had to deny who I was as a person.

Religious roots run deep in my family. My maternal grandmother's first marriage was to a Pentecostal preacher at 14. She eventually escaped that union and went on to marry a Southern Baptist preacher. Her grandmother was also a faith-based Pentecostal. There were quite a few preachers in my grandmother's lineage, but these women all had a special bond of their own.

They were seers.

My great-grandmother had a gift, her mother had a gift, her mother had a gift, and her mother had a gift. By the time the lineage got to my own mother, she was afraid of what that gift represented. So she did what a lot of the women in her family did. She didn't marry a preacher, but she turned to religion and shut that part of her down.

I was taught from a young age to have a deep and meaningful relationship with Spirit, Source, and God – however you choose to identify it. I've since branched out from what I thought were the limitations of what those specific words mean to me, but at the time I was trying to reconcile what I saw and knew to be true and what everyone else wanted – *even needed* – me to believe.

This confusing struggle put me under so much stress that it began to take a toll on my body. I developed stomach ulcers at eight years old. I was eating myself alive with guilt, shame, and fear. By age 21, I had developed heart palpitations and suffered from constant and debilitating anxiety attacks. I was racked with angst and depression over what I knew could be possible in the world, but also as an empath, I could feel everything. However, because of the way I was taught to wire myself, I didn't realize I could tune to that. I couldn't grasp the idea that I was like a remote control being able to tune in to other things. I was just automatically setting my frequency to tune in to all the negativity, to tune into all of the bad. I felt like I had no control over my body, my emotions, or my own energy field. I felt constantly bombarded and perpetually burnt out. As I continued to grow, in came the anxiety and depression, and my heart began to give out. As I lay in my bed, I remember believing,

"If I don't do something different, I'm going to die."

That was ultimately the realization for me that I was not living my life. I was living the beliefs of my parents, the church, and society in general. I was living everyone's ideology but my own.

In my reality, I could *see* the quantum field. I could *see* energy and angels. I could *see* behind the thoughts of others when they were searching for a missing word or idea. I was like a computer programmer looking at a computer code and saying, "Oh, there's a one and a zero missing here." For people, that one or zero might be missing in a relationship. It may be absent in their health. I could literally see into their fields and see how everything was unfolding. I was taught, however, that what I was doing was not something a person should have the ability to do. As a sad result, this created deep spaces of real trauma inside me that I internalized.

I recognized I was not created for this misery. I knew I was not put on this earth to suffer and die. The people around me were saying, "No, no. That is what you were created to do. Life is suffering; you suffer, then maybe in the next life you'll be rewarded."

I knew I was living someone else's life. So I thought, "Well, if this is not my life, what is? WHO AM I?"

That was my first step. I knew it was a big question to ask right off the bat, but it needed to be answered.

Who are we beyond our stories? Who are we away from our thoughts and illusions of who we are? We are not who our racing mind tells us we are. We are not our pasts or shadow selves.

We are so much more.

The number one thing that holds us back is the idea that we are somehow separate, that we are somehow "less than." We think we are distanced from the unified field. We think of the collective consciousness as the field, and that's not necessarily the case. The collective consciousness is in some ways the ego of all of us, the ego being the individualized presence. If we did not have our ego, we would all walk around OM-ing and living on mountaintops, believing that everything is beyond wonderful. However, we would not have an honest understanding of who we are as individual experiences and presences of Source Energy. Now, the ego in this instance is not a bad thing. It is simply what gives us our individual identity. Sometimes when the ego takes over, that's when it can become a golden opportunity for us to shift.

Currently, what we call the "collective conscious" can also be called the collective "un-conscious" because it is a bit unconscious at present. It is not particularly awakened at the moment. We do not see it awakened in the area of politics, the monetary system, or when we turn on the news. In most cases, that is what we think of as the collective consciousness. But there is a deeper collective conscious that is connected to Spirit and moving freely in the world and the unified field.

The unified field is the space where if you take a high-powered frequency beam microscope and put your hand under it you can see through your hand. We do not see into nothingness. We see the unified field. To put it into cognitive terms, it's the feeling you get when you walk into a busy Wal-Mart on Black Friday.

You feel nervous, rushed, and frenetic. You experience it when you enter a warm, welcoming home for a dinner party and feel immediately at ease. What you're feeling is the charged energy from someone's personal field.

We all have a personal field as well, but we tend to separate our personal field from the unified field. The unified field is a place where no matter what you plug into it, everything from your personal field is automatically neutralized.

The unified field is your *I AM* presence – the origin of pure source energy. It's about creating what you truly want. Any negativity in your field that you were drawing to you through cords you had with other people, ideas that you picked up, or spaces that had been passed down to you generationally can be dissolved. You can define your free will and be exactly who you are by announcing, "This is who I am, and this is what I choose in this moment." You then move that energy into your personal field and out into the world. By allowing ourselves to tune in and harness the essence of who we truly are, we are unleashing our power to create.

As we go through this journey, remember that you are infinite possibility living in a field. We want to turn that field into the infinite possibility of pure love, pure source, and pure divinity. This is not the divinity you may have heard of before – the divinity where you have to adhere to a certain path, or submit to the demands of others, or feel any form of shame or guilt. Those are the mental stories that keep us separate and in our suffering. Those are our ego, our mind trying to keep us "in line." If you're willing to let those stories go, and rewrite new narratives with acceptance, compassion, and the energy of peace your possibilities and joy are endless.

MEDITATION

Are you willing to let go of the things that have kept you in a box?

Are you willing to lose the story and choose freedom, love, and joy?

Are you willing to be your own seer and trust your own voice?

Resist the urge to separate or isolate in times of sorrow, grief, or hardship.

Bathe in the unified field that is always there to comfort you and bring you home.

Be willing to dwell in the infinite field of possibility.

Be willing — even if it's just for a brief moment of now — to choose happiness over all else.

CHAPTER 7

THE FREEDOM OF FREEDOM

H ere's something to ponder.
What is one thing you'd like to create in your life?
Think hard.

If you could manifest anything you truly wanted, what would it be?

Let's say you want to relieve your debt. You want money, but not because you've formed a weird attachment to paper with pictures of people and numbers on it, or that you think Benjamin Franklin is one sexy dude. You believe money buys you freedom. You desire the *energy* of freedom.

Why do you want the energy of freedom? Because in freedom there is joy, there is lightness, there is abundance.

What does abundance feel like?

Freedom.

What does freedom give you?

The ability to open and unleash the "you" you truly are – the joy of pure expression.

Perhaps you're looking for something else. You may want relief. In my story, I suffered from heart conditions, PTSD, agoraphobia and many not so great things at an early age. I often said, "I want to feel better," or "I want to *be* better." What I wanted was relief. I wanted relief from pain and fear. Relief from anxiety and sorrow. But *why* did I want relief? I wanted relief because I didn't want to be experiencing what I was experiencing. I wanted to be free.

There was a time when I was saying, "I don't want to feel this way." But by adamantly stating what I *didn't* want, I was blocking myself from having what I *did* want and need. I thought the mental dam I was building would keep my pain and sorrow at bay, but had I pushed the barriers down and let life unfold, all that I hoped for would flow into my life.

When we say, "I don't want to feel this way" we're actually saying is, "This is how I feel. No! I don't want it, I don't want it, I don't want it!" But the irony is when we focus on the "No" that's what we're asking the Universe to give us. You're saying loud and clear, "Give me more of that!" If we allow ourselves to, at that moment, press pause and say, "What do I really want?" The answer is,

"I want freedom."

Freedom is an opportunity. It's the free pass to ride the euphoria express – our ticket to joy.

If you are in a relationship and you're saying, "My partner isn't honoring me" what is it that you truly want? You may want out of the union because the relationship feels tight and constricting. You want something that feels freeing. You hunger for the freedom to explore who you are, the "You" without restriction or limitation. The "You" embodying your truest expression. The "You" overflow with joy.

In everything you want, you can go back to the feeling of freedom, joy, and happiness. It may feel a little like cheating, but there's a place where we can have that right now.

There's a point where our ego kicks in and decides that things have to be perfect before you can be happy. You can't be happy *until...*

"I can't be happy until I have a long-term partner."

"I can't be happy until I have more money."

"I can't be happy until I lose 50 lbs."

It's mostly a laundry list of things you have little or no control over. And that's where you give your power away.

But what if in the moment of "right now" you gave yourself permission to think past the obstacles you feel are before you and only see the joyful abundance?

You may have debt. What would it feel like having the freedom of being debt free?

You may be "single and NOT loving it" right now. What would it feel like to have a caring, supportive partner?

You may feel that you're not supported – at work, in your friendships, or with your family. What would it feel like to live in a supportive world?

What does it feel like to be free, supported, the debt paid off, to have a loving partner, what does it feel like to have a job and be surrounded by co-workers who like and support you?

Let it all sink in.

You are beginning to create the vibration of sovereignty, bliss, and wonder. You've started to change your fundamental vibration and change your entire system. You've picked up the remote control and turned your vibrational channel. The Universe sees this shift and says, "Oh. They're no longer sending the signal, "Go away, go away, go away." They're no longer vibrating at, "I need, I need, I need," or "I want, I want, I want, I want." They're now vibrating on a calm, peaceful level. So, let's give them more of that calm, peaceful energy."

That's what starts to change the outer reality. That vibration is what begins to lift off the junk that you've been struggling with all these years.

So often, as we grow up, as we grow *out* in the world, we define stillness and love as an escape energy. We want stillness and love because we want to escape the chaotic world and return to stillness and love – back to the feelings of God. We feel unmoored and vulnerable, yearning to be tethered to *Source* again.

It's easy to get lost in a sea of doing and chasing and running. Like swimming against a riptide, you can get sucked into a sea of despair by thinking how great life "could be" or how things would be wonderful "if only…" Before you know it, you've been tossed and turned, drowning in confusion and weighed down with "I'll be happy when…"

We need a reminder that the energy inside us – the energy of everything – is all we'll ever need. It is the compass that guides us home. Even if in the chaos of life, you get turned around and forget who you are, you have the power and presence to call upon this energy to lead you back to the actual source of stillness and love. You don't have to escape to find your freedom. You can go back to this energy; you can *be* this energy and carry this energy into the world. This force allows you to feel and be the strength, the presence, and embody the stillness and love the world so desperately needs.

What is one thing you'd like to create in your life?

Whatever it is, it's already yours.

MEDITATION

I know that I do not have to be, do or have anything to experience love. While my conscious mind may tell me otherwise, I am choosing, in the moment of now, to open to Pure Source and allow in a new thought, a new vibration of feeling what it would feel like to be whole, loved, and complete in every moment. From this vibration, I know that I am now allowing my new inner world to manifest as my reality and outer experience.

CHAPTER 8

PASSION & PURPOSE

There's an old joke about a businessman who finally retires and is on vacation in Mexico. He sees a fisherman pulling into the dock and asks if he will take him out fishing. The fisherman explains, "Sorry, Señor, but I am done for the day." The businessman looks at his watch and says "But it's not even noon yet." The fisherman says, "Yes, I go out and fish for a couple of hours. Catch a few fish, and then I come back". The businessman tells him that's hardly a way to run his business and asks what he does with the rest of his time. The fisherman says, "I wake up late. Go out fishing. I come back and have lunch with my family. I play with my children. Then take a siesta. Sometimes we go into town for dinner and I sip wine and sing and dance with my friends late into the night."

The businessman was stunned and decided he would help the fisherman out. He explained that if the fisherman applied himself more, he would do better. The fisherman asked how. The business-man says, "First you should go out all day and catch all the fish you can. Maybe even go out again at night. Then you would have enough money to hire a crew. You'd make even more money and reinvest it in your company. After a few years, you could buy a fleet of ships. In no time you could be catching so many fish you that you will need to start your very own cannery. Why in five years, you could become the biggest fish company in Mexico. I bet in twenty years you could be selling your fish in stores around the world. Then when you turn sixty, you could retire like I did – a rich, rich man."

"And then what?" says the fisherman.

"And then you wouldn't have to work another day in your life. You could buy yourself a nice home in a sleepy little town like this. You could wake up late, go out fishing, and have time to play with your children. Maybe take a siesta and sip wine and sing and dance with your friends late into the night".

The businessman slowly walked away embarrassed.

This joke is hundreds of years old and has been told around the world with Zen Buddhists and Russian farmers subbing in for the fisherman. But this resonates with a vital message of the impor-tance of knowing what we want to be in life and the most direct way to be it.

One of the questions I love to ask people (especially ones deal-ing with money issues) is, "If money didn't exist, what would you do?" The first thing most people say is "NOTHING! I would lie around all day and do nothing." I used to say that too. We all dream of the day we could be that fisherman just spending the day relax-ing. But is it really what you would want to do? It was fine for the fisherman. That is what he loved, but after a while I think most of us would get bored with going out to the boat every day and fishing. We would have traded our computers and desk for a net and a bucket of bait, but it would still be a job.

Another question I love to ask (this time to people dealing with relationships) is, "What would you do if you were going to live for another hundred years?" Sometimes when we are stuck in relationships, we feel like, "Well, we've done it this long. We might as well stick it out to the end." That shows where you're locked into your finiteness of this reality. You're not allowing yourself to expand and explore. You aren't living your life with passion.

I can hear your ego screaming, "Living my life with passion? I would just be happy to live my life and feel okay." However, that is exactly what has kept you from moving forward. You were aiming for okay and seeing this as a destination to be achieved. You were merely crossing a finish line to finally being happy.

Like the businessman, you're looking for a goal, not a purpose. You move from small improvement to small improvement. "If I could just make a little more money." "If we can make it through the holidays." You are seeing each step as getting closer to a point in your life when you will be happy. Like the businessman, it was one step at a time, and still he wasn't fulfilled. I mean, here he is on a beach in Mexico and he is trying to tell a happy fisherman how to improve his life. That poor businessman may never find happiness.

I asked the questions:

"What would you do if money didn't exist?"

"What would you do if you would live for another hundred years?"

"What would you do if you had plenty of energy and were completely recharged?"

I know, right? Those questions are surprisingly daunting and can be a little scary, because there are so many choices we have in front of us.

Sometimes we can't think of just *one* choice and get so overwhelmed it short-circuits our brain. It's like getting too many emails at once, and your server shuts down. There are so many ways we limit ourselves through what we think is possible that we are not open (even though we think we are) to what we truly desire. But when we start to "feel into" those questions and begin seeing our existence as more and infinite, we are allowing ourselves to see our "I AM" presence that continues forever. We plant the seeds of excitement that will birth and create that reality. We create ourselves in a whole new way.

The funny thing is once we release all our restraints and the fears we are running from, we realize what we want to run to can often be the same things. When we go from a mindset of, "I wish I had more time or more money" to "I have abundance and all the time in the world" we shift into an astonishing space of inspiration. Where I used to say, "I would like to do nothing for the rest of my life," now, when I have a day off, I create ten new things. There is a part of me that longs to expand. It's not that I'm incapable of doing nothing, but somehow doing nothing always turns into creating even more.

I had to be at a point where I thought I was going to die before I could hold the vibration of everything I wanted to be. The universe was just handing me my own limitations, and I was experiencing them and thinking, "The universe is an awful place. Why am I being punished?" Now, on the other side of it, I realize I wasn't following my passions. I was following what other people wanted them to be. I had sent myself these obstacles to go in the right direction. I saw the dead ends and collapsed bridges as punishments instead of road signs and detours trying to get me to go where I needed to be.

To where I could live my own passion.

The businessman spent his life trying to achieve his passions while the fisherman *was* his passion. It reminds me of a quote from one of the most passionate men in history.

> *Be the flame, not the moth.*
> Giacomo Casanova

MEDITATION

In this moment, I direct and allow all I am to begin revealing, step by step, easily and effortlessly, things, events, people, and spaces in myself that I am passionate about.

As these passions arise, I choose to allow myself to feel at home, filled with purpose, as inspiration and action become one with all I am, in peace and love, made manifest through-out my inner and outer world.

I love myself.

And so it is.

CHAPTER 9

YOUR ULTIMATE REALITY

This may sound funny, but I have very wise tea. They are Yogi teas, and I often drink more than one of them every morning. Each tea bag carries a message on their tag, just a few words of wisdom to brighten the day. Today's words of wisdom were, "Live In Your Strength."

Interesting. "Live In Your Strength." It made me think, "What is my strength?"

Many people think they must battle in life and work harder on their journey than anyone else. They feel they should put in an enormous amount of struggle and long hours to get what they think they want. But life doesn't need to be a struggle, and it doesn't have to drain every drop of energy from your veins. If you're going through something that seems to be insurmountable, remember *you have the power to change.*

So how do we take the things that seem the most difficult or painful, and bring them into love so we can fully be healed and living our divine purpose?

Stoic writer Seneca said, "Every new beginning comes from some other beginning's end." He's right. It's a shiny sliver of space in us where we allow completion. As we allow for that completion, we open the doors for all the new we're inviting. We usually come to this work because we are looking for a big life-changing event or just looking for our life change.

Often, we're so focused on a life change that we focus only on the wrong in our life. Many times we associate strength, whether it's physical strength or mental strength, with our ego and who we are. But we are so much more than the totality of who we have ever thought we are. The person you think you are is the sum total of the experiences you've had. The person you can become is only limited by those stories of who you are.

As you open to new potentials and possibilities as to where your strengths lie, also heed the message of my second tea tag,

"Love Your Soul."

This begs the question, "Who have you told yourself you are? How have you allowed your parents, your teachers, your spouses, your children, your friends, your colleagues at work, your communities, to define you? In the greater picture of your life, how have you been living a life based on someone else's desires or expectations? How have you made your life a series of boxes, checklists, or categories, and allowed yourself to be defined by an idea of what you should be, rather than what's in your heart?

Or are you inhabiting a space of living in your strength, from the open heart, defining yourself as love, telling yourself, and telling the world who you are, through the lens of potential and uplift-ment?

One of the ways you can move back into your own identity and power is to practice love and compassion. It's not the kind of love and kindness where you subjugate or sublimate. It's you. It's where you forgive yourself for not knowing what you didn't know years, months, days, or even moments ago. It's where you stop beating yourself up for past mistakes, disastrous relationships, and places where you just didn't act from your highest sense of awareness. You can allow yourself to give that over to something more significant.

There's a phrase, "Let go and let God." So many of us have stories who or what God is and maybe, like myself, you've had experiences growing up where God was turned into an energy that other people used as a form of abuse or control, so you have closed off your heart or your connection to the universe. But, by "letting go and letting God" you free yourself from the people, labels, and baggage, that no longer serve you and allow your most divine self to guide your path.

You are the embodiment of freedom. You are love in action. When you open up to that, then you open yourself up to your divine right energy, which is living your passion as your most authentic self.

So many of us struggle to find our passion. People ask, "What is my passion? What am I here for?" The thing to know, which can sometimes be a difficult idea to embrace on our journey, is that what your passion is today may not be what your passion was several years ago. As we allow for our passion, we also allow for who we are to change. This change can sometimes be met with resistance. Beware of the space of the ego, the individualized presence of who we are with all our stories, the part which separates us from God. The mind has sectioned itself off and made itself its own ruler, and it wants to *know*. It wants to know what came yesterday, what's coming today, and what's ahead for tomorrow. It wants to control and put everything in a box so it can problem solve and keep everything nice and tidy.

When we get into a space where we can let things go, when we allow life to flow, we can access that passion again. At that moment, when you are feeling alive and feeling connected, nothing else matters. But we hear the voice of our ego telling us, "That feeling doesn't mean anything. You have to go be better." We all have that voice that tells us "no". I had that voice that would particularly say, "You know what? You suck. You don't belong here. You're a freak. Nobody loves you. This stuff you're doing, and feeling doesn't matter. You better stuff it. You better hide it. You better literally break yourself and do something different -something that matters in the eyes of other people because this is worthless. You're worthless."

This is how we buy into the lie of limitation. This's how we accept the illusion of misery and begin shutting ourselves down. When we're in the feeling of connection, of feeling joyful and whole- when we allow that to come from the open heart and connect with love? That feeling is everything. That feeling is what begins to align us with our true purpose-to experience ourselves as divine love. Our real purpose is to experience connection, worthiness, love, and flow. The more we allow those feelings into our lives, the more we permit the inspiration to take action steps to manifest and create our ultimate reality.

What *is* your ultimate reality? We talk about wanting a life change. We want change but what does change mean to you? Change for so many of us has been what we need to do to get where we want to go, but *right here* is where we are and where we *need* to be in order to create the next step.

When we release the need to be anything other than what we

are, we open to acceptance and responsibility, which in turn, opens us up to flow. The flow then carries you in often-unexpected ways, and it allows you to feel loved, and to feel good. It carries you to a space of feeling better about who you are. By feeling strong and connected you've opened to moments of inspiration, and you find yourself taking action. You suddenly look back, whether it's two days, two weeks, two months, or two years and realize, "I'm a completely different person. All because I faced my fear and opened up that one space."

Kung Fu Tzu said, "The journey of a thousand miles begins with one step." Maybe your mission is only a few blocks. You may be very close to where you want to be in life, but all you need to do is take that one step. That's all there is. Once you open to the energy of love and support, the egoist, separate energy that says, "No! You must be, do, have, control, push, and pull! I'm being held back energetically from this, this, this, and this!"

We must stay active and connected. "Am I willing to let go of that? The ego? The drama?" How willing am I to let go of all these voices that have held me back for so long?"

We have the power to transmute the density that holds us back. Everything is energy, and we can move the energy that keeps us locked in an ancient holding pattern. If you pull back the layers that have been covering you for so many years, the brightness and the clarity of you shines crystal clear.

As you begin to release those burdens and let go of all that's been weighing you down, you start to feel more of who you are. You feel more grounded and in control of your life. You feel rooted in. You feel unified, and you start to feel safe in this world. In feeling safe, you can remember, "All the things that I thought were terrible about yourself, I allow myself to be forgiven." At that moment you allow yourself to reconnect and love yourself. All of these levels and layers allow you to shift into someone completely new. Your heart opens, and you begin to experience the open vessel of pure love. It's in this ascended heart that everything you are is embodied and realized as pure, peaceful, source energy.

MEDITATION

I am letting things go, things I've been holding for too long, so that I may let life in.

I'm ready to take the first step on the journey of joy, discovery and, inspiration.

When I'm in the feeling of connection, of feeling joyful, of feeling whole, I am free.

When I want to let go of an old belief or story, I will "let go and let God."

CHAPTER 10

THE HERE & NOW

If you've seen the movie "Ferris Bueller's Day Off" you caught the teen's romp around the Art Institute of Chicago. Cameron, Ferris's best friend, finds himself alone in front of the pointillist masterpiece by Seurat, "Sunday Afternoon on the Island of La Grande Jatte." The camera shows the wide shot of the sprawling canvas filled with finely dressed revelers, sweet children, and a few random dogs. The camera pans in closer and closer to the painting, zooming in to show each tiny brush stroke, and each infinitesimal dab of the paintbrush. The close-ups are intercut with shots of Cameron growing uneasy as he focuses in and loses perspective, no longer seeing the big picture, only the tiny, barely observable dots.

The director John Hughes said, "I always thought this painting was sort of like making a movie, the pointillist style. You have no idea what you've made until you step back from it." It can be said that life works the same way. We become obsessed with our irritating specks and forget to step back from it and see the incredible beauty we've created.

The world is always changing, and sometimes history repeats itself. Take, for example, America, which has grown and changed dramatically in its relatively short life as a country: The Civil War, The Industrial Revolution, The First and Second World Wars, The Dustbowl Era, The Civil rights struggles of the 50's, The Vietnam War, The Stonewall riots and LGBT rights coming into the mainstream in the 60's. Welfare programs, Medicare, Medicaid. Globally, countries have gone and are going through these same struggles at different times. But if you look at America decade by decade, you can see that even though there was an immense struggle, there was also love.

Throughout her existence, you can see there has been war, but there has also been peace. That peace brought new challenges, new possibilities on the horizon and those new possibilities meant further expansion. When we look back at our history, we can see that we're also in a tumultuous time in this decade. Things have sped up so rapidly with the Internet that it everything seems magnified and more urgent. We're in a position and a place where we see the world unfold in new and sometimes frightening ways.

In the 1980's, participants in the Cold War thought we were approaching the end of the world. Americans in the 50's were building bomb shelters in their backyard. People in 300AD thought if the sun went down at night it might not rise the next day. The energy we all feel – the same energy that was stirred by the 1968 riots in Chicago, the 1890 Massacre at Wounded Knee or Nero's reign over Rome in 64 AD – is essentially politics. The energy has evolved and changed shape over centuries, but at its base core, it's an ancient energy of control, deceit, greed, and power.

While there are clashes all over the world, there is still considerable change afoot. Cultural change is the reflection of a changing society, and the shift happens when someone steps forward unafraid and creates something new. Michelangelo, Da Vinci, Picasso, Miles Davis, Elvis, The Beatles, Madonna, and Lady Gaga all brought something new to the world even when the world was on the brink of turmoil and significant change.

We are a group of people who came together with an intention to live from the heart and to create a new life for ourselves and to create a new understanding of ourselves. If we're afraid to go out and share who we are with the world because we're worried we're going to get a little skepticism thrown our way, we're never going to be the change we want to be.

We're not living from a place of power or ego. We are a part of the love vibration that lives forever in everyone. We are a part of the love eternal. We're showing ourselves and shining our unique beauty. Don't be afraid to step out, to fail, to do something new, because your light is going to live forever. You are laying the groundwork and setting the stage for all that is to come and all that will ever be.

As we shift and grow, our resonance evolves. We open up dimensionally to new spaces and gain a unique perspective on our life that we may have never experienced before. As the inner camera pans out, we see how our journey has unfolded and continues to unfold. We have a bird's eye view of where we stumbled, took a wrong turn, and now where we can embrace our adventure fully – where we get to choose it, be it, live it right here, right now, and in our full power. You are in a place where you can say; "I create my life now as the light of me. I let go of all of my attachments and chords past and present, and I direct *Source* to bring all of that, balanced into the light so that all of me is 100% committed to my life right now. I commit my higher self to unity with all that I am, bringing all of me here in this moment."

No matter the state of the world, don't be afraid to shine your light. Don't be scared to step out and be seen. Don't be afraid to fail. Your love, your light, your essence is going to live forever, and in that living forever you are laying the groundwork. You are setting the stage for all that is to come and for all that will ever be. By being here, we've enabled a space that if all of the chaos is rolling and has reached a critical mass, we've disconnected from that. We have now created a space and place where we are allowing ourselves to instill massive amounts of love into the world.

We've pulled back the camera lens so we can see the massive canvas before us, primed and ready for us to use every hue to create our masterpiece. We've allowed love to be the paint that colors our world, and we'll only fully understand what we've made when we step back and see it here and now.

MEDITATION

I belong in the here and now.

I am here to shine my light and ignite the world.

I am here to live it fully from my open heart — with love, hope, and kindness.

I see the giant canvas; I know the beauty of being a piece of the whole.

I see myself in every dot, every brushstroke, and I am grateful, because I know I am both the painting, and the painter, and through choice, I get to experience whatever I desire to focus upon.

CHAPTER 11

CHANGE

What if you had to wear the same set of clothes every day, for the rest of your life? Sure, you may have loved those jeans twenty years ago, but now they're too small and they're cutting into your waist. The shirt that was once your favorite go-to top may be too tight, too loose, out of style, or just plain falling apart. These clothes are literally binding you to an old vision of yourself and halting your ability to expand. While these garments worked well for you at one time, the truth is, in many ways, you've outgrown them.

What if we were wearing the same emotions, the same reactions, and the same energy every day? Even though we wanted to change those aspects – and maybe we've even spent years and years trying – what if there were things in our energy field that just kept on creating the exact same responses, like electrical impulses in the synapses within our brain, our body, and our cellular memory? While it may sound silly or strange, most all of us have these places, where we constantly put on the same expectations, the same reactions, and the same beliefs about what's possible and what's not possible.

Just like the clothes, we begin to be seen as those very same reactions and beliefs. They are being mirrored back to us, and through our brilliant minds, which seek to self-validate, we keep ourselves in a loop – like a hamster on a wheel – moving and moving, but stuck in place.

Our thoughts and belief systems all have a signal. They have a vibration, a frequency, and a resonance. We keep carrying those old beliefs around, like Charlie Brown's friend Linus and his ratty blue blanket. Even though there's a time when we outgrow the need for our own security blankets, it feels weird when we begin to let them go. Being without our "blankets" makes us feel vulnerable and unguarded. We feel naked without them, so the mind keeps finding reasons to keep them around.

Subconsciously we say, "Wait. I know I want to grow into a greater space, let go of my 'blanket,' change my old beliefs, and step into the next phase of my life. I know I'm ready for a miracle." However, there's a space – a new version of us – which that miracle would create that is so new compared to the vision that we hold for who we are in our energy bodies (pituitary, our pineal gland, our third eye), that we self-sabotage.

Even though we want to shake things up and create something different, it's such a new place that the newness becomes uncomfortable and we find ourselves subconsciously moving *backward*. It's the old "two steps forward and three steps back" dilemma. You go on a diet and end up gaining weight, or you finally get your health in check, and you lose your job. It's the spaces and places where we begin to hide sabotage within our energy. Outwardly it feels so uncomfortable, yet there is an inward, almost psychic draw that pulls us right back to where we started.

Let's get real here. What is the actual reason we fear change?

Change can cause severe stress and anxiety even when it's spawned something incredible. Let's say you land your dream job. After the initial celebrations pass, you begin to panic big time. "What if I can't handle it? What if they find out I don't know what I'm doing?" The newness of this change and the unknown that lies ahead makes you fearful and nervous because you don't want to fail. You don't want to be humiliated. You don't want your every insecurity, perceived or real, to be exposed. Then there's the big one.

"What if I fail like I've failed before?"

One of the most self-defeating issues that come up in our energy fields is guilt over what or how we've created in the past. As we begin to understand how we create on a deeper level, we start to feel guilty. That guilt is one of the most prominent roots for all blocks of creation. We simply feel guilty about who we are. We feel guilty for having too much. We feel guilty for not creating enough. We feel guilt around our bodies, our past, our family, and our perceived mis-steps or mistakes. We tell ourselves we aren't smart enough, worthy enough, deserving, or even capable enough to create, have, and maintain all we desire.

This is where a very important truth comes into play: "Your thoughts are not your ever-lasting truth." Yes, even the thoughts and beliefs that have been hanging around in your psyche for decades. They are not your truth. As a vibrant and creative being, you can set a new vibrational level, a new space where you allow yourself to eliminate any lower vibrational cords or attachments, release the past, and welcome real change. You have the ability to build up a new energy field and bring in the healing love and frequencies that empower you and aid you in your expansion.

There can be an unconscious desire to invite in the frequencies or energy that sustain your old stories and keep you on the hamster wheel, especially when you're under pressure or facing the unknown. Pure source and pure energy allow you to accept that you are the Divine in action and that you are whole. This understanding lets you lift the lid off of any and all boxes you feel you've put yourself in and free yourself from anything past or present that holds you back.

There's a statement I use, that came from a program called "The Big Shift" that I created along with a friend, and these can be your words too, if you like.

> *"I am committed to one happy, healthy, prosperous,*
> *abundant whole and that makes me happy.*
> *It's easy, simple, quiet, and complete,*
> *now and consistently."*

I use those words because I am committed to wholeness from the perspective of divine love. That space is one in which I allow myself to be whole as I am, free from cords or attachment…there is no need to fix self or other and there is freedom in that realization. Every individual is sovereign and whole, no matter how the exterior circumstance may appear to our ego. When we come to that truth, we can detach from any need to save or fix anything about us or in others. When we can release that, we free that space within ourselves to begin creating and shifting from a space of ease. Choosing to have the shift be easy and create happiness, wipes away all "need" to hold onto righteousness or the need to be right. Simply put, it allows us to flow.

Choosing the path of opening up and being our authentic self means embracing change. It takes courage, heart, love, trust – all of which we already have at our disposal right now. We're all doing it. We're all changing and creating even though we don't always acknowledge it. In fact, you may feel the exact same today as you did yesterday, but at some level, moment by moment, you chose to hang on to beliefs or reactions – even if at a subconscious level. So, while you feel the same, you have actually created an entirely new experience of an old story.

Letting those stories go, becoming conscious of just how powerful our choices are, allows us to make new choices. We can choose to commit to our happiness and wholeness, knowing that as we become more happy and whole, we can then choose to remind others that they too have this choice. This choice is the energy of pure source; the energy free of any belief you have about the judgment, the being-ness or the getting there. We are free to choose love, and we are free to love who we are, which through Universal Law, begins to create more and more love and joy in our lives.

MEDITATION

Today, I ask that I be shown my choices. I am committed to seeing clearly and truthfully who I am, while loving myself and letting go of resistance and judgment. I allow myself to see my choices — whether I call them "good" or I call them "bad" — because in seeing them, I free myself to redirect and to choose anew.

The very first choice I make, as I step into this new awareness, is the choice to know that I AM WHO I AM right now, based on choices I have made. I choose to not judge those choices, but to love them, thereby freeing me of any cords or loops. I choose to see myself clearly, through the eyes of Source, and know that all things are truly possible.

CHAPTER 12

ANGRY OLD MEN
IN AIRPORTS YELLING AT TELEVISIONS:
A Love Story

L ately, as I've travelled, I've noticed an interesting phenomenon I like to call "angry people yelling at televisions." And it's not just in airports. I've seen it in restaurants, at family gatherings and even riding the bus! Maybe they can't help themselves. After all, from their perception, there may be a lot to be angry about, a great deal to be concerned about and even more to be scared out of your mind about. I've seen these folks stare at the television screen silently for long stretches of time; contemplative and absorbed only to hear them let out an expletive laden rant that makes even the coolest business traveler spill their Café Mocha all over their latest copy of Forbes.

It sounds strange but there's something these older gentlemen desperately need. Yes, these men who've "seen a thing or two", been around life's proverbial block, worked a job not for years, but *decades*, watched the moon landing, saw JFK shot, and risked their lives in WW2 storming the beach at Normandy.

These tough, weathered, respectable men need nurturing.

They're missing nurturing at a deeper vibrational level. They're missing the love. There is a piece of *them* that's missing, a space that does not feel safe to express in this world, so they shut it down. They feel they have to control, and the only way they can control is through the means that they know how. When those means shut down, they have to fight *against;* against their peers, against the press, against the government, against the family of raccoons making a home in their back yard! Anyone and anything. Their idea of patriarchy is threatened. Their sense of identity, self-worth and purpose is all in peril, and it's terrifying. We as a society are beginning to recoil and shut down as well. We too are afraid of the unsettling change and disorder that's coming to pass, so we hide out in our shell and give the TV our own expletive laden piece of our mind.

Between the chaos and the perpetual newsfeed, we feel everyone *else* is causing chaos, failing miserably, and sending us all to hell in a hand basket. What we don't realize is that *we're* misfiring too. We're going about it all wrong. We're projecting our anger, terror, and emptiness onto other things; politics, injustice, weather catastrophes, violence and unrest. We want to stuff up our emptiness with the very things that are keeping us unfulfilled. While those events are important, they can be a dangerous distraction that brings more sorrow to our inner selves. But by going in and filling ourselves with nurturing energy- the energy of being loved, of being held, and of being protected and taken care of- even if it's only by ourselves, is the true salve that heals us and makes us powerful again. So many of us don't feel taken care of out in the world. So we fill our own heads with worst-case scenarios, and we worry. Whether you're masculine or feminine, you need that nurturing. Without love and self-care, the "you" you think you are remains in a state of paralysis, yelling at the television and shutting down to stop the pain.

Fear can make your life small. Worry can rob you of time and energy. But you can choose to a life of joy, self-love, and purpose beyond your imagination.

What's going on under the "YOU" you think you are?

If you could choose right now to have anything, do anything, be anything, what would you choose to have and do and be?

What would you choose to let go of?

"If I want to live free, I'd have to let go of my spouse, my kids, and my job."

What are the limiting beliefs about your job, your spouse, your children, or your money? What are the limiting beliefs you would have to let go of so you could choose to have everything and not limit yourself? How could you still enjoy everything you have and allow all those things to support you on the journey of who and how you want to be?

You not only have the potential, but the power to create potentials and possibilities in every single moment. You have that potential and power to create those possibilities through allowing yourself to realize that every single opportunity and every single moment, you can simply set down your stories, your fear and your fervent need to rail at a television set. What choices can you make to let go of worry and limitations that would allow you to not shut down and allow your overall story to change so things could come in and support you?

There is sadness around choice. We think, "What am I leaving behind? Am *I* being left behind? Who am *I* leaving behind?"

The truth is no one is being left behind. *You're* not being left behind. Angry older gentlemen are not being left behind. Everyone is connected. Everyone is always in his or her own space – nurtured, loved, and sovereign.

Someone once asked me, "Jarrad, how can you always have that positive outlook?" I said, "What's the worst that can happen?" Obviously I want to be here. I don't want to go anywhere. If I had it my way, I want to stick around and live this life as long as I can and have a good one. The worst that'll happen is I'm going to die and hopefully it's not an awful thing. But once I'm there, it's okay. I'm home in *Source*."

If that's the worst that can happen, what are we truly worried about? We can let our fear go. When we realize that outside time and space in this life, time and space are an illusion. This might sound weird and kind of woo-woo but we're already there. We already exist back home in *Source*. From that perspective, we can realize there is no one on this planet that we are ever leaving behind or that is getting left behind. In that space, the deepest part of where we feel the sadness, no one gets left behind. There's nothing to get back to because we're already there.

Love has welcomed us in.

MEDITATION

When we feel sadness or fear, it can also be where we're start-ing to unify with our whole self.

We can feel from the individualized presence, a place where we've not made those choices before.

Start to experience the overwhelming presence that has always been there for you throughout your life and begin to release the emotion that comes up.

It includes sadness as well as being loved. When you feel the sadness, allow it to be there, but realize you're allowing it to open up to a greater love.

Open your heart. Feel it all. Let it wash through you.

Let your whole self unite with whole source and be reborn.

Repeat after me: I am Loved. I have not just the potential, but the ability to love myself, and in this moment, I am choosing to do so.

CHAPTER 13

FEAR

When I was much younger I would hear people speak so joyfully about how great they felt by being "born again" through various religious or spiritual experiences. They would go on and on with such jubilation about being so happy and "feeling new." Since my religion taught me that I was basically a walking freak show, I wanted to throw those people off a rooftop. The younger me didn't believe people could be that happy. I couldn't envision a life that could ever be that wonderful. At the time I was a very pessimistic, negative person.

I was born into a family that, like most families, had some "stuff." I was able to feel and read energy. I could also see people that had passed on. Coming from a conservative, religious household, I was taught that my abilities were not something that should be shared openly with people. I was taught to keep my gifts hidden away for fear of scaring people or provoking ridicule. Everything

I possessed was very wrong in the context of how our family functioned in society through religion.

Each day, I meet so many wonderful and beautiful people who, through various life experiences, have been taught to hide their light under a bushel. And in some regard, many of us have been shut down in different ways at some point in our lives. We've allowed our luminosity to be snuffed out – whether it's through the misunderstanding of others, the anger of others, or someone else's old wounds acting out. We've all experienced that situation and the after effects of being branded as broken or wrong can take many forms. For me it began manifesting itself in massive weight gain and heightened anxiety. While those issues could be attributed to my own inability to process my gifts as an empath, it also came from being taught that who I was as a person was just simply and inalienably *wrong*. This reckoning caused me to shut down my heart.

As I grew a little older, I worked at shedding some weight. But the more I began to lose the pounds, come into who I wanted to be, open up more and more to myself, the more my health deteriorated. I was trying to improve one thing, and losing out on another. I was convinced I was dying. Every day I'd say, "This is it. Today's the day."

It was an awful existence. I was depressed, anxiety ridden, and suicidal. Nothing I did seemed to work. It was in a space that one day I finally woke up after being in bed for a close to a month – too afraid to do anything and feeling so awful that I decided, "I give up. I'm ready. I want to die."

But the thing is *I didn't really want to die*. I just wanted the world to hurt less. I wanted to *me* to hurt less. There was enough of an understanding within who I truly was and who we all are, that no matter what kind of injuries or abuse we've been through, there is still a space in us that vibrates and resonates with the love of pure source energy. In that space of giving up, I opened up to my authentic self just enough to where I think, "If I'm going to go, what would I like to do before I die?"

What I wanted to do was go to California. I wanted to see the ocean. I thought, "I'm going to do something different. I don't care if it kills me, because I'm already dying." I made my arrangements and off I went.

As I entered the airspace of Los Angeles, I began to feel different. I didn't quite know what made me feel that way, but I could feel a slight shift. At this point I was still having three to five anxiety attacks a day, but when I got to California everything changed. I felt like Dorothy in the Wizard of Oz, trapped in a black and white Kansas and opening the door to a Technicolor wonderland. There was so much energy that I could *see* colors. When I say 'colors' I don't mean, "I looked at a tree and it was *more* green." What I was experiencing was much more powerful. I could actually see people's auras. I saw things in people's belief systems that I had never seen before. I was very sheltered growing up so I thought there was a finite number of belief systems available to people. But the vast array took my mind to a whole new level. The more auras I saw the more belief systems I saw. I realized that these belief systems were just energy, and if we could shift our energy, we could open ourselves up to shifting belief systems.

As I began to shift my own belief systems about who I am, what is right, what is wrong, what is God, what is heaven, what is hell; I began to open up and realize we are all one. One energy made up of everyone. We are all acting though our own experiences. We're either shutting down who we are or acknowledging who we are, or engaging in interplay of both. As I opened up to those ideas my guidance became much stronger and I was able to see other people's energy as well as my own. I was able to recognize in myself more clearly what my core beliefs were, what ideas and concepts were passed down through my family line, what I picked up through my own life lessons, so I began to move that energy and shift it dramatically. Soon after that, the medications waned. The anxiety stopped. The depression stopped. I got down to 155 pounds through exercise and watching what I ate. It wasn't a difficult process and it happened quite quickly. I had conquered something I had battled the first twenty plus years of my life and as a result, my whole world changed.

Having endured that experience I got to a point where I had to ask myself, "What do I want to do and who do I want to be?" I thought, "If I have to get my doctorate in divinity and metaphysics with all that I know and all that I've done, I can do that. If I have to go work in the food court, like I've done in the past, or if I have to work in retail sales, which I've also done, I'll do it. I'll do what it takes because I want to stay here, I want to continue to expand, and I want to do what is right for me and who I am."

After making that commitment, I really didn't have to do anything. Everything started back up on its own. Years later, even when there was a writer's strike, instead of wallowing in nothingness and lamenting my lack of a job, I looked at it as an opportunity to write about what I knew and tell the world the things that had yet to be told.

All these years later I am where I am today. I have three best-selling books, a wonderful group of people around me, and I've never been happier.

I think if my 25-year-old self had met me at 36, 25 year old me would have wanted to punched 36 year old me in the face for being so happy all the time. I was in a place of hatred, but what

I didn't realize is that the hatred came from a space in me where I was not allowing myself to open up. I was incapable of tuning in and tapping into all I wanted and the seed of hatred grew from deep frustration.

At a higher vibrational plane any hatred we display is actually fear. Whether it's born of fear, sustained by fear, or living with fear it's the energy of fear. Whether fear inhabits our alter egos or our shadow self in our energy bodies, there's still a part of us that knows who we truly are. Thankfully, that part of me was still there. It called out to me and made itself known though the darkness. I could barely hear it but it was there. I know some of you haven't heard it in a long time, but that voice of truth and light is still there. If you can still hear it, the mind, the ego, and circumstances can come into play and we begin to feel disconnected. We begin to plug into the part of us that no longer knows if we are safe, that no longer knows that we are loved and no longer knows there's abundance. We begin to feel that in order to have things, we have to struggle. We start to feel the "us versus them" momentum and feel alone, uncared for, and abandoned.

When I was 22, I was at the height of my belief that I was wrong. There are many people who ask the same question whether they're 22 or 62.

"Why aren't I moving forward?"

What happens at the wider levels of self is through past lives, templates, religions, and stories but if you look at archetypes through human history, there's a very engrained encoding template that conveys, "We are not supposed powerful. We are not supposed to create." So, whether that message was communicated or insinuated through religion or experiences, when we step into our power for 99.9% of people a little switch clicks on that says, "I'm scared to death to be here. I don't know if I can handle this." We begin to fear that everything's going to be taken away from us or we're going to lose it all. It translates into, "I'm not supposed to be here. I don't belong." This translates in every facet of life. That's what happens when relationships dissolve or jobs break down.

There's a space in the third energy dimension, which is the physical reality, the way things have been for thousands and thousands of years. But when we talk about the fifth dimension where feelings are the fuel – the manifestation and the engine of everything that is. That is how you manifest. It's through feeling. It is the intent and excitement of the pure, open heart.

Take a deep breath and feel into not "what it would it have to be", but "what would I have to do to fix what I don't like?" That is actually what keeps us stuck. Now ask yourself: "What would it be like to be free?" If you were free, whatever problems you were having with your job, your relationship, your finances?" If you're free and you're feeling free you must have done all the things to get to a state in your being-ness where there's freedom." You're broadcasting out to the Universe that says, "Send me more peace." As you begin to receive more peace, everything in your life begins to mirror what's going on in the inside.

Life is an expression. You are an expression of source energy. You are here. You are right now. What you're wanting so often whether its love, or money or a career, it's going to change your life. So often we want what we think it will bring but we're not willing to undergo the transformation. The transformation is painful. It feels like your whole world is falling apart.

But the wonderful thing is you can let the whole world fall apart, while you're undertaking the beautiful upheaval of creating the new.

MEDITATION

Right now, I am choosing me. I choose and allow myself the love and the joy — and the space — to break the cycle and know deeply that I AM the experience of divine love.

I Am beauty.

I Am health.

I Am the energy of abundance — even when I don't know it.

I Am joy.

These are not just words. They're vibrations and energy.

They are frequency and experiences that are available to me whenever I Am ready to connect, and right now, I AM!

CHAPTER 14

CONTROL

I meet people every single day, from all walks of life, who feel like they are unable to grow as human beings. They feel unable to expand – stuck – and have a deeply rooted fear of being left behind by the world, by their loved ones and even by their own bodies and minds. It's not always something they would consciously associate with energy of abandonment, but often times, it is a more profound recognition that situations are shifting, and not in a way that makes things better for them. It's a fear that the rising tide of uncertainty will be the death of whatever control they have (or think they have). The illusion of control – however real it feels – is the only thing keeping them afloat and alive and that is creating substantial geopathic stress – the connection between earth energies and their effect on people's health and wellbeing.

We, as universal energy, are continually expanding. The ongoing barrage of what we see as "troubling events," both personal and worldwide, have caused an extraordinary amount of turmoil, struggle, and strife energy. The focus on that energy perpetuates more duality, which then creates a larger manifestation of the very thing we don't want, but can't seem to turn away from. Thus, at both a collective consciousness and individual level, many people in the world today are experiencing a deep anxiety and a fear of losing control.

If we look back through the last several thousand years of history, we see control, patriarchy, suppression, oppression, and violence all associated with the term "power." Judging by what we're witnessing at present, those vibrations of aggression and fear have never truly been addressed or gone away. This is why, at a genetic core level, its imperative we direct our body to hold a new energetic charge of knowing that the universe is a safe place and of knowing that we are infinitely loved. This shift in perspective or both self and other is the change which can create a new world.

Power is an interesting word, and it has a lot of baggage, for most people. In the purest, *Source* sense, it simply means knowing at a deep level, just how loved, connected and creative you are. It is the ability to turn the probable into the possible and manifest all you are through expression of love (love being the byproduct of the deep connection associated with the empowerment). However, for most of history, this is not what power has meant, and thus, collectively and personally, we have created or inherited stories about what power is, what we have do or sacrifice to gain or keep it and who may be coming for us once we attain it. It has become something "outside" of us.

Throughout history, we see stories of people stepping into power, and then somehow, in some way, losing it, abusing it, having it taken, or having it overtake them. It is a story we all come by quite honestly. The way it plays out today, collectively and at the individual level, is that when others gain their sovereignty, anyone who is afraid of being replaced or unloved conveys the energy of "I have to control you. If *I'm* not in control...." Fill in the blank. From, "No one will love me, and I will be abused and cast aside," to the fear that we will destroy others or ourselves.

We see these dynamics play out in every walk of life, from Shakespearean kings to schoolyard bullies. It's the place where people act from that lower vibrational space of needing to control due to a fundamental lack of self-love.

When we consider our own struggles to stay in control, it often seems like an unconscious act. Constantly trying to manage every situation, to keep our cool, and to get a proverbial "grip" is exhausting, not to mention fruitless. Meanwhile, we desperately long to find a solution on how to escape the need to have our fingers in every pie and always run the show.

But here's the thing. Want as me might, sometimes, control is a limitation. It comes from aspects of the ego which "needs" things to be in a certain order, go a certain way, or be just so. We keep defaulting to it because there's a deeper place in our energy field which says, "I'm not sure I have enough energy to do this." By "doing this" you mean give up the need to control, or trusting that you actually create your own life. You feel if you relinquish control it will be like managing the most beautiful crystal glass shop with everything in precise order and nothing out of place then unleashing a bucking bronco loose inside.

There is a positive side of letting go of control, which is knowing and trusting that the universe and source always have you covered. But, in order to bridge to the space between a clenched fist and open palm, we need to clear the energetic space. The control freak in you feels if you let go that bronc is going to rip loose and leave chaos and devastation in his wake. Everything will descend into madness, and you will have to do nothing but pick up the pieces. If that's your belief and your energy, you're not going to give up control. You'll spend the rest of your life just trying to get back to zero.

Have we gotten to a point in our world where the need to control actually controls us? Sure, we all have dreams, desires and aspirations, but when does the need to run the show cross the line into ruining our lives?

When I was younger, I heard a story about monkey poachers in Africa. They would tie sacks of food to trees, with holes just big enough for an empty hand to slide into. When a monkey would reach in and grab a hand full of food, their closed fist would become too big to pull from the sack. They were trapped by the very thing they thought would sustain, feed, nurture, and help them continue their lives. Had they just been able to let go, they would have been free.

Lao Tzu said,

> Can you deal with the most vital matters by letting
> events take their course? Can you step back from your
> own mind and thus understand all things? Giving birth
> and nourishing, having without possessing, acting with
> no expectations, leading and not trying to control: this is
> the supreme virtue.

The need for control is not just about getting what we want. It's also about getting what we want NOW. Often times, when we're striving to control a situation we want it to be a solo job. We don't trust others to live up to our standards so we choose to cut out the middleman and make it happen *our* way. That's why most people with control issues find delegating tasks and working with a team sheer torture. We have a plan- *our* plan- and nothing should get in the way of our plan. Our deep-rooted fear of the unknown takes hold, and we choose to force things to happen instead of letting life expand.

The waves of the ocean are mighty. They're so powerful they can carve away at solid rock. Humans, try as they might, do their best to barricade the sea, but you can't build a wall against the ocean. Ask any hurricane survivor. You can't control the sheer force of nature.

If you're trying to make the sea bend to your will, you're fighting a losing battle. You have a choice. You can try to swim against the tide or learn to surf and go with the flow.

We can't control everything and everyone. And ultimately, that is probably a good thing. But, we can change our perceptions of others and develop a new relationship with ourselves and with the world, wherein we can open our fists and behold the possibilities we didn't even realize were present.

MEDITATION

Take a deep breath and say, "I am not responsible for every-thing that happens today. I am ready to release my need to control anything or anyone. I am listening to the rhythm of my breathing, my heartbeat, and even the voice inside my head. My I AM presence give me the space to slow down, be peace-ful, and honor myself as love.

Live with your heart and you will always be home. I can feel the warmth of goodness and wholeness without the need to judge it or challenge it. I can just be it.

No second-guessing. No fear of making a mistake.

I can embody love and stillness. I have the power to let things unfold as they are meant to.

I can exercise passive responsibility; control without controlling.

I can be my true self.

I can be at peace.

I can be free... because I AM.

Chapter 15

HOME

From mud huts to mansions, we all crave four walls and a roof – a space to unwind, relax, and sometimes, even escape. It's been a long week, and you step through the threshold to your place. Maybe you are greeted at the door by a loved one, a room-mate, or a family pet. Off come the shoes and coat. On goes the TV. You plop down on the couch, put your feet up and relax. Whew… you made it.

We need a home. If for nothing else than a place to keep our stuff. It smells like us. It vibrates with our energy. Have you ever noticed how strange your home feels when you have a guest stay over? Or how alien and empty it is when a loved one has passed? We can be sensitive to even the smallest change in the home. You can feel a shift in the energy before you can pinpoint the actual physical difference. But you can feel it.

The home is our cocoon where we come to heal and surround

ourselves with that familiar and familial energy we need. It is our protector keeping us safe from the rain and snow. Keeping us safe from things that go bump in the night. It is the one place we might feel safe. It is sometimes the only place in the world where we think we belong. But like anything else, it can become too much of a good thing. We can become addicted to it.

Cocoons are great forces of transformation, but a cocoon is meant as a temporary place to for a caterpillar to absorb energy and morph into a beautiful butterfly. Our home is a place for use to feel safe and surround ourselves with energy to heal and recharge. It's the place we live but it's not the place where we do our living.

We get addicted to the physical trappings of our possessions. We start to feel a more significant connection to things than to people. Now with the Internet, we don't need to leave the house to talk to friends or order food or see the world. The world comes to us, and we don't even have to wear pants. It's as if the caterpillar decided not to emerge and spread its wings but stayed safe in the cocoon to binge watch Netflix. The butterfly denied.

At the same time, we are always growing. We are still connected to the energy of the universe and we crave abundance. But here's the thing. Abundance always means change. Abundance IS change. You can't tell the Universe, "Please, I want to grow and have love come into my life, and to achieve my potential...but keep my life exactly the way it is now!"

At what point does your home stop being a place to keep all of your stuff and turn into a place to keep all the great stuff away from you? If you lock yourself away from all the terrifying things beyond your doorstep, you're also locking yourself away from all the tremendous things that *are* waiting just for you.

If you haven't made the connection just yet, I'm not only talking about our physical spaces, but also about the home you make inside your being. Your *sense* of home. The individuation of energy that is us.

When we get hurt or have trauma in our lives, we put up walls to protect ourselves. We feel we need them to protect our energy and allow healing to begin. We put locks on the doors and only let certain people come inside. The guest list gets smaller and smaller as we lose trust and give in to fear. Our fear leads to more hurt, so we build thicker walls. We buy bigger locks. More fear. More hurt and on and on and on. Eventually, we have locked ourselves in and all restorative energy out. We cut ourselves off from the flow of the universe.

Even after we heal, it may not be an immediate renovation. It can take time to break down those walls and ultimately break through. We might even tell ourselves we are ready to open up. We are prepared to share ourselves. We go through the motions, but we haven't truly accepted the energy we need. So, we find we are wearing that spectacular new dress as we are troweling a new level of bricks on the castle wall. Or we have decided to buy a new suit that we can wear while we are digging another moat.

To accept the energy, move forward and evolve, you need to leave the castle. Take yourself out of your comfort zone. Lower the drawbridge, and run in the empty field for a while.

You are going to find that while you spent all of this time staring at the cement walls and iron bars that "protected you" from the creatures in the big, bad woods, you actually cut yourself off from a majestic forest. You traded an enchanted garden for a moat and barb wire fences. You haven't made yourself the King of Camelot; you've made yourself the Prisoner of Azkaban.

You're free. Give yourself a full pardon. Explore and connect and reconnect. Accept all the new love and energy you are finding.

Home is where the heart is.

MEDITATION

I know that Home is where the heart is and right now, I am allowing my heart to expand into new lands, while knowing I am safe, secure, and deeply loved. I choose to live form this energy, knowing I am the creation of me, in a new, whole and loving way.

CHAPTER 16

WHO AM I?
Family & Genetic Beliefs

Who am I?
Why do I believe what I believe about both myself and the world?

I know we're getting kind of deep right away, but I pose these questions so you can start to receive the truth about who you really are. Most of us, had we been born in another time or another land, or to another family, would be very different people. Yes, there is an aspect of us that would remain the same, but our belief systems would be vastly different. We might hold different views on politics, religion, gender, and yes, even self-worth. When we realize this, we begin to see just how much of who we are has been defined or programmed based on other people's beliefs.

Don't get me wrong. I'm not saying we are victims of circumstance or in any way suggesting that we are not responsible for making our own choices. In fact, I am saying the opposite: by understanding who we are AND why we are, we allow ourselves to step into the ultimate space of self-empowerment, because we return "choice" to our own selves.

We don't just define ourselves based on our own collected belief systems, either. We also project those beliefs and perceptions onto others in our lives, creating a walking, talking and living embodiment of our own expectations.

Via our perceptions and beliefs, we collectively create the general rules of conduct for our lives and what we deem appropriate for others. Through our society, our culture and our family system, we create, indoctrinate, and ultimately accept or reject what we define as "normal."

When we are babies, our parents are like gods to us. They are literally all we know. We depend on them for nurturing, for cleansing, for substance – physical as well as mental – and so much more. They have maximum influence on who we are and our outlook on life and creation, as a whole. This is why so many people get triggered by their families. After all, who better to push your buttons than the very people who installed them?

We come into this world with a very strong attachment to Truth. Look into a baby's eyes and you instantly feel possibility. You feel an infinite sense of love. You feel a reminder of what "home" is. Yet, as adults, we then set about "teaching" our young what it is to be human. We never stop to think 'why" human is what it is, or exactly who or what determined the rules.

We teach our children the fundamentals of society, just as they were taught to us.

Think back to when you were younger. Did anyone ever tell you "Oh, that's just your imagination?" or "Stop playing around"? Did you ever receive messages about staying small or not celebrating yourself? "Sit down and be quiet!"

"That's not important right now!"

Much like clay in the hands of an artist, we begin to take shape based on our surroundings. But, beyond what we see with our eyes or hear with our ears, there is more of which to be aware.

How many times have you heard someone say, "Oh, she is just like her mother," or "Like father, like son?"

Just as we receive genetic markers from our birth parents – physical traits such as eye or hair color, height, etc. – so too do we "inherit" their energetic characteristics.

These are our *genetic beliefs*, the things we have learned from our heritage: our parents and ancestors, through both spoken vibration and through nonphysical form. These beliefs are not just things we have learned in this lifetime, but genetically and energetically, they are things we have absorbed and taken on. We have it pointed out to us all the time. Someone will say, "Oh! Your grandmother acted just like that" or "Your grandfather used to love/hate the same thing!" There are places and spaces in our human experiences where we have simply taken on other people's stuff.

Scientists have even done studies on what they call "epigenetic inheritance." They have shown that memory can be passed down through our RNA (Ribonucleic acid). Several mice were put in a chamber with the strong scent of cherry blossoms and then given an electric shock. They got to the point where they associated the smell of the flowering buds with pain. Over time, the scientists found the test mice had children and even grandchildren that were born with a fear of that same odor.

There is a phrase used in ancient texts, and if you are religious or come from a religious family, you may have heard this phrase: "The sins of the father are visited upon the children." Energetically, this is epigenetic inheritance in action.

Imagine saving up for your dream home, only to arrive on move in day to find that the previous owner never took any of their stuff. What if they not only left their things, but they expected you to use those things, instead of choosing your own.

Sharing a house or apartment with someone is difficult, let alone a room or even a bed. But with family, we often find little elbow room, physically, mentally, or emotionally. Even when we leave the nest, we take the programs and buttons with us out into the world. The buttons that were once pushed by mom or dad now becomes a manifest loop where we don't feel valued at work, or where we create disharmony in relationships, or lack in finance.

When we are in utero, we are fed through an umbilical cord. That cord is meant to nourish and provide for us; it is there to give us life and keep us safe. As we emerge into this life, while that cord is physically severed, energetically, we begin to form cords of another kind. We start forming "ties" in our fields to our communities, which usually begins with our physical family. We form cords running from them to us, from us to them, and like umbilical cords, these energetic ties are meant to nourish us, to create a flow or balance within this new energetic eco system to help us know our place and validate our newly forming belief systems. As we grow, we often realize that rather than mutually supporting each other, these cords have created dependence or co-dependence, where we find ourselves feeding off of one another. We get caught up in the trauma and drama of the other person. We are tied to them and often become tangled up in our shared history, repeating patterns and wounds, because subconsciously, this energy is feeding a belief system put in place long ago.

This is when we can choose to find our own light. We can choose anew and open to discovering the space to unify and amplify the love of who we are, as *Source*, free from any cords or programs.

What if I told you it was possible to drop the cords, open your heart, and feel love for yourself?

A friend was once teaching a healing seminar and a woman approached her with tears in her eyes.

"I will do anything to heal this pain I feel," cried the woman.

"I want to let this go. Please. What can I do?"

Without missing a beat, my friend, quite the intuitive herself, zeroed in on an episode of abuse which had occurred in this woman's life. She shared what she saw and who she saw.

"In order to truly heal and let go… in order for you to move on and create what you desire, you have to forgive them."

The woman's eyes glazed over with rage.

"I will NEVER forgive them."

Unfortunately, many of us have a lot in common with this woman. We have a desire to be right or righteous, and we place that above our own desire to be happy.

What if forgiveness meant you could consciously create anything you desired? Are you truly ready for that responsibility?

Energetically, we often hold on to these cords from our families, because we don't believe we are ready. These cords are like safety blankets, and even though they weigh us down, and keep us ensnared in trauma and drama, in some way, shape, or form, they keep us safe.

But what if happiness was a choice we could make? What if that choice were enough to clear our spaces of everyone else's "stuff?"

Through the lens of forgiveness, we allow ourselves to be who we are, and we allow everyone else to be who they are. We can begin to view our families as their own "I AM" presence and realize they are on their journey just as we are on ours. This goes even further into our "family" of man. Can you begin to see everyone as Source sees them? Are you willing to allow that every single person on this planet is a living, breathing, belief system, created through their own histories, and realize that in this truth, you free yourself to become your own programmer?

It doesn't matter if you are 7 or 107, you are always a child at heart, born purely of Spirit, and no matter how far down you may have buried your essence or forgotten your Light, you can still tap into what you truly are.

Ask yourself:

"What would it feel like to have the most amazing, most giving, most wealthy, most nurturing and most infinitely amazing family ever?"

As best as you can, let whatever story you have around family go. Start to play pretend and "re-create" your past. What might it have felt like to have been born into a loving, supportive, nurturing world, where you were up-lifted and encouraged at every step?"

How does that feel?

That feeling is the frequency to tune into.

If the old tapes start to play, tell them to go take a nap. This is your space. This is your choice. You can release every single cord in your life by knowing that you are Divine Love. You are not just Divinely Connected to All That Is, you are a living, individuated expression of that very energy and love in action.

Feel what it would feel like to be welcomed into an eternal state of connection and love, free of any limitation, wherein you have choice to choose whatever you desire, and where every feeling, thought, and emotion is birthed from this space of love.

Welcome home.

MEDITATION

I know that in this life, I have given my power away — sometimes to my physical family and sometimes to the family of mankind. I have created stories that I know my ego has lovingly sought to validate and sometimes, I recognize those stories have kept me in lack and limitation.

So, right now, I am choosing to forgive everyone in my life, myself included, that I may release all cords. As the spaces and places in me which needed nourishment, fill in with Divine love in action, I now choose to know that I am choice and love in action and that I am home and whole, within All I Am.

And so it is.

CHAPTER 17

EGO & ALTER EGO

E very one of us has the similar morning ritual. We wake up, go to the bathroom, then stare in the mirror and prepare for the day. We might put on make-up or shave or brush our teeth and hair. We put on the face the world will see. But before you make yourself look presentable and ready yourself for the day, do you ever really look at the person in the mirror?

For centuries, Zen monks would meditate on this simple koan riddle: "What was my face before I was born?" They refer to this as our "original face."

Or if you like to rock out with your meditation I will quote a 70's British rock band, The Who:

"Who are you? Who, who? Who, who?"

As we look into the mirror, we may notice the wrinkles around the eyes, the beard stubble or the extra pounds under the chin, but we never really see ourselves. Those are just the outside physical parts of our person. They are elements of the mask we wear. Inside is the energy that we use to define ourselves – the electromagnetic pulse in our being that holds the charge of our identity. This is the "whole brain." It is that part of us that combines all the energies we're made of and individuates us from source so we may learn from each unique experience.

At our core, we all hold an energy. We tap into it for strength. It is the original energy; a touchstone we may use to center ourselves and realign with the universe.

It would be pointless for everyone to be identical and have the same energy journey, so we have created individuation for ourselves. Each of us has chosen a different frequency that is specific to us and will shape our personal experiences and our sense of identity.

This is our Ego.

It's almost as though we have chosen to forget so that we may learn. The Ego is our conscious thought. It has sectioned itself off from *Source* and has a constant need to know things. It wants to know what is coming next and to organize what has been. It also remembers and holds onto all the old stories and scars of our past. It wants to put everything in a neat and tidy box to study and it defines all of these things as "who I am."

It's not malicious. The Ego is just doing its job. It is there to rationalize and problem solve. We use it to translate for us. It takes the energy of the unfolding universe and translates it into physical emotions. While it may slow things down, it is meant to be there, so that we can learn and analyze what our life is.

There is the other side of Ego, though. The Alter Ego. It's not quite as kind. The Alter Ego is that part of our brain where we fight against that which we truly desire. It's like a malicious virus in our computer system that is continuously running in the background. The Alter Ego is the voice that taps into emotions like fear and anger. It is the build-up of negative stories that the Ego has saved. It is the voice of our embarrassments, our pain, or our resentment.

It's like two computer programs running at the same time. The Ego might say "I want a relationship and abundance in my life." And the Alter Ego remembers past breakups and failures and says, "I am not worthy", "I will have to work too hard," "If I find love I will be giving myself away." It will think of a million reasons why you shouldn't achieve your desires and will use shame, guilt and panic to steer you far away from them.

Spiritually, the Alter Ego would rather we not even know about Source. Those times when you might have felt touched by that energy, the Alter Ego will send waves of messages saying, "You are making it up," or "That wasn't real, and you didn't change anything," or "You don't belong here." It sows distrust inside us. For some, it's genetic religion telling us that this is the wrong path. Some people have felt betrayed by God in the past or associate him with control, abuse or have a complete mischaracterization of what it is to feel that love. For others, it's a fear of what they would do if they connected to that much power- perpetuating a distrust of themselves.

This is all a form of genetic deceit where we don't allow ourselves to open up to what we truly are. Because the voices of the Ego and Alter Ego sound an awful lot *like* us, or are indeed coming from us, we begin to think of them as us. It's as though we're staring into a mirror covered with fog that doesn't let us see us for who we really are.

We need to wipe clean the mirror so we can see our sovereign self. You need to experience the cleansing picture of you at Source. Wipe away the guilt and history and physical imperfections. Ask

Source to be physically shown those places where we experience love free from shame or guilt.

Tell the Ego it doesn't have to know what is happening next. It doesn't need to hold on to past stories. It doesn't need to be the control freak. If you see something on TV that brings up negative emotions and feelings that don't seem to resonate with your energy, you need to turn off the TV and go into another room. Go into a space of unity where the Ego and Alter Ego aren't running the show and allow yourself to tap into Source.

This is what is meant today by being "mindful." Yet, the irony is, you are really taking the old paradigm of the mind out of the equation. Being mindful actual engages the heart and allows you to step back and see you vs the mental stories, persuasions and perspectives held by the ego and alter ego.

The more that we practice being in that space and let the flood of Divine Love, Unity, and True-Self energy into our lives, the more we begin to shift, and we begin to notice the fog on the mirror washing away. We are left seeing ourselves for who we really are, and as we look into that clean mirror, we are able to rejoice in what we see.

MEDITATION

Just for today, just for now, I am opening to what it would be like to see myself through the eyes of Source — beyond any stories of guilt, shame or physical judgments. I choose to invite in the energies of Love, so that I may begin to see myself as who I truly am: Pure Inspired Source in Action!

CHAPTER 18

TRIGGER HAPPY

I don't want to face this pain.

I wish I could get out of this marriage.

I want to love myself, but I can't.

Why can't this be easier?

There are so many instances in life where we wish we had and "Easy Button" Something we could hit to make difficult choices, money troubles and conflicts within our own mind be quickly and effortlessly resolved.

The office supply chain Staples started this idea as an advertising campaign to show customers how easy it was to utilize their print services and access the availability of their vast amounts of supplies. They even created actual Staples branded "Easy Buttons" for people to keep on their desks to remind them, "Hey! We can make things so much easier for you", which in corporate speak translates to, "Hey! Come buy our stuff!" When you hit the Staples

Easy Button, know what happens? Nothing.

We all want the Easy Button for; let's face it, everything in life. We want to be able to press a button and have our difficult situations dealt with. But the great irony of life, energy and Creation is that we *are* *t*he Easy Button. *We* make it easy or *we* make it hard.

As we tap into our energy source, even if we don't know it consciously, our bodies begin to recognize the spaces and places where we're pulling the pain from within our energy field. Our job is to open up to use this energy, see ourselves for who we truly are and ask, "Can I love myself? Can I see everything I've created and can I allow it in my life? Can I give it a space? Can I let go of the resistance knowing *not* letting go doesn't mean it will stay with me forever? It means I am no longer in resistance and no longer pushing it. This gives me the space to move out of reaction and into pure creation."

At a larger level this is the space of knowing yourself and loving yourself and merging the two together. And, as we move through this gateway of powerful energy of support we meet "The Unmet Self." We begin to not only meet these spaces within; we begin to integrate these spaces. We begin to become one with these places and open up to our wider self. We begin to see why we've created these places and how to love ourselves through that process. Through this powerful integration, a lot of our trigger energy is processed out and released along with much of our genetic energy that's been holding on through our family.

Genetic beliefs are a big part of why holidays around families can be so triggering. Every family member has a specific role that they, at some point in time, be it in their childhood, early development, or even in adulthood, have taken on to fit a certain space. That identity has been literally integrated into their being-ness saying, "This is my identity. This is how I function within this family unit."

There's an old saying that states, "You have to take the prophet out of his home city for him to be the prophet." That's because it's so difficult to go back into that space where everyone has projections and they're putting them onto you. Then you begin plugging into the old patterns and before you know it, you're acting like you were before you knew any better.

At a greater level, we're also talking about spending time with all of our own energy. We often have hidden triggers within ourselves that within our daily lives we run into and we get triggered and we don't even realize we're triggering ourselves.

You may feel you've made so much progress with your family dynamic and your past. You may think you're made great strides in areconciling your past. You think, "I got this. I'm not the least bit worried. It's aaaall cool." Then BAM! There I am with my family. BAM! There I am in my hometown. BAM! There I am driving by the house of my girlfriend who dumped me at the Homecoming Dance.

These energies come up no matter how present you are or how much work you've done on yourself. No matter what, the energies will emerge. You may think you were long over something, but the memory and the energy bring you right back to your sophomore year in you older brother's hand-me-down suit with a carnation in the lapel and a broken heart under your freshly ironed shirt.

When you feel blindsided by the past or triggered by old patterns, just breathe. Take a conscious breath and ask yourself, "Who am I?" Because ultimately in that moment, and every moment is a new moment, so, in that moment you are asking yourself to come forward as the creation that you are. To remember that, "I am that I am." To remember, "I am the direction of my energy."

One of the things that can happen when we find ourselves in that position is that we forget that we are sovereign and we plug back into someone else having the power over us, or we plug back into wanting to control or be controlled by someone else. You think, "Well, my identity was wrapped into this," or "Their identity is clearly still wrapped into that so, who am I to take their identity away?"

The new thing to do is understand that yes, this person is also sovereign, but they are not sovereign over *your* creation. You are the one who gets to put out that you are – resonating like radio frequency broadcasting from your energy field. You may have sent out a signal 20 years ago and it may have taken them 20 years to signal it back to you. But know in that moment, it's not about you. It's about them. You are not defined by their song.

The brighter you shine your light, the less you feel *forced* to shine your light, and you can allow yourself to *be* the light. You're free to emanate the peace and love that allows people around you to shift as well.

You are not who others say you are. You are not who you family says you must be. You are not who you were.

You are pure golden light – always new, brilliant, and uniquely you.

There do not have to be fingers on the triggers ready to pop off at any time. When we wave the white flag and make peace ultimately everyone is happy.

MEDIATION

What would it feel like to feel connected, not just to you, but to Source?

The energy is always available to you.

It mirrors back to you the truth of who you are.

Not the old stories. Not the limitations but actually awaken-
ing inside you: the vision of who you are.

The you that is divine love.

Light that up in your energy field. Light that up on your whole
body. Knowing, "I am whole. I am love."

I release the need to tune into anyone or be tuned by anyone. I
know that I am the direction of my light right now, and in this
moment, I choose Love.

CHAPTER 19

BIRTHING THE NEW

Have you ever woken up in the morning with a gut feeling you just can't shake? You know there's more to life than what you're living now, but you don't know what it is or how to get there. You feel a passionate urge move into something new, something that gives you freedom and abundance. But, beneath your burning desire to embrace the now, you're clinging to the old.

Let's say you're talking on your cell phone with a friend. Your phone is in call mode and you're talking on the phone, but in the background, new posts are popping up on your Facebook feed and Candy Crush is waiting patiently for you to link three peppermints in a row. Like your phone, your vibrational frequency may be running fears, feelings, thoughts and belief systems in the background of your psyche that your conscious mind does not recognize it's playing. And those programs are a massive distraction.

We may think, "It's okay. I'm tapping into the infinite potential of The Universe, and it's all good." While that may be true, through that funnel, our underlying, dominant frequency has a set resonance or trigger point, and the Universe is simply a wall socket. We are plugged into that energy, yet it is feeding *all* our apps, old and new, pre-installed and ones from our past we forgot you ever installed.

Energy is energy. It doesn't judge, it simply powers up whatever apps we are running through our vibrational resonance. In other words, you receive your own inner world manifest in the outer world.

Our own physical nature and energy fields are in desperate need of a reboot. It's time to consciously refresh our thoughts, our feelings, our past relationships, our old patterns with money, who we are, and our relationship with Spirit. We can attain the widest alignment within ourselves as higher spiritual beings: to be a wider being of light, open to the experience of the oneness, the wholeness, and the unity of love consciousness.

There's a great deal of fear around "becoming whole." If we feel we are not whole, we are unable to adequately accept what is and accepting what is the birth canal for happiness and brand new creation.

To allow yourself to move vibrationally into a new space of clarity, you must remember, "What you resist persists." There's a big difference between someone saying, "No. Thank you." and "NOOOOOOOOOOO!" The energy of "No. Thank you." is just that. There's no attachment to it. But the latter is emphatic and filled with emotion. You are exhibiting massive resistance, and as long as you are pushing away from something, you are creating a magnification of the frequency of no.

To welcome new frequencies to be born, you have to be in a

place where you can release the fearful "fight or flight" response and accept what is. The fear of releasing that resistance is feeling, "I'm not whole." It's then when your frequency feels the need to reset to "push or pull" mode and you revert to running you're worn out background apps or plug into your old beliefs of, "I'm not supposed to be in this job, this relationship, this planet. I need to push myself into a new space."

It's not that you don't belong where you are. It's not the Universe trying to squeeze you out of a position, push you into poverty, or shoehorn you into yet another space that doesn't fit you. It's ultimately coming from within. Some part of you is screaming, "I'm not whole!" The Universe is simply answering what your frequency is broadcasting. It's answering the frequency of "I'm not whole."

If your true desire is to birth new happiness and new creation, you must begin by accepting exactly where you are. Birthing something new does not mean leaving something behind. Everything is flashing light. It's all just frequency in motion. The light of the cellular energy is always blinking, always moving. From one second to the next we are continually moving into a new moment of now.

We are transforming in every second even though most of us are creating the same picture over and over and over again. We believe we're establishing a trail which gives us a history, a story of who we are, an identity. As we begin to birth something new, our ego, the aspect of us that gives us an individuated idea of self as separate from ourselves, from others and from source. When we declare, "I would like to create something new," the ego rears its head and replies, "You are now threatening my identity. You're threatening who I feel I am!" But our ego doesn't die.

It evolves.

We are in a constant state of birthing the new. You can absorb your power, ground into that source and allow yourself to say, "This was my story before. Here, in the moment of now, even if it's just for five seconds, I'm going to allow myself to acknowledge that everything before was a past life."

Ask yourself, "Who am I *right now?*" We think new thought is new thought, but a lot of the new thought is simply a new understanding, a wider understanding, or a mystical knowing of a deeper and more genuine wisdom that has been with us for a very long time. Your knowledge of who you are in the moment of right now is always flowing and constantly changing. As the Greek philosopher Heraclitus says,

> *The river I stand in is not the river I step in.*
> *For it is not the same river, and I am not the same man.*

Creation is never about tapping into or tuning into something else or someone else and drawing from a false source. It doesn't borrow from another power system. This is about you opening up to your frequencies, your world, and your potential as a creative being and understanding that everything is energy.

Everything moves according to your highest vibrational offering – the vibrations beyond the story of you. It's the space and the place, the levels and the layers of belief simply peel back and allow your true essence to shine forth and give birth to the new.

MEDITATION

In the moment of right now, I allow whatever puzzle pieces I may have been working with, to change.

I know that as I change my inner resonance and choose new feelings and perspectives, I open up to the new pieces, and indeed a whole new completed picture.

I choose to allow all I am, and all energy to support me, as I consciously choose to birth myself anew.

I am reborn, now!

CHAPTER 20

YOUR MONEY STORY

I had been living in California for a few years when my voice-over career started to really pick up. I was happy. I was making money, and I felt abundant. Then, as fate would have it, there was a writer's strike and all of the commercial work I had been doing dried up. I was blindsided. I had no work for almost a year and I felt tremendous guilt and shame. The bills kept coming in, and as a result, I racked up $90,000 in debt. I never thought I'd find myself at that point. I went from flying high to a crash landing.

Even though I was in the red, I kept participating in personal growth programs thinking the right one would help catapult me out of my situation. I looked at every program as a winning lottery ticket thinking, "This is it! This has got to be the one!" While each program I completed brought me a step closer to meeting that secure, sovereign space in me, I knew deep down I wasn't ready to become the manifestation of wealth and abundance I wanted to be.

So how do we get there? We need to learn to embrace abundance and money without fear, guilt, or animosity.

What is money?

What does it represent?

We have this idea that money will bring us freedom. We believe money buys us time, comfort, safety and happiness. But money doesn't buy you anything.

In fact, money doesn't even really exist. We trade value for value. Worth for worth. With the belief that only money will solve your problems, you're stating to the Universe "I can't be free until I have money!" So the Universe responds,

"Huh? So, she believes she's not free, but she wants money. She believes she's not free, so I'm not really sure what to give her. Should I bring her more stuck-ness? Should I bring her money? If she needs money to be free, that means she's not free. I could bring her a little bit of money and throw stuck-ness at her at the same time. Sure! Let's do that."

As you cut through the ballooning cocoon of financial fantasies that have enslaved your thinking for so long:

"Money will give me power!"

"Money will make me happy!"

"Money will bring me love!"

You soon realize your heart's desire is not money at all.

It's freedom.

Think about where you're currently free in your life. Feel into that deep aspiration.

"I know that I am free. I know where I am loved."

Dive deeper into the desire and ask yourself,

"Where am I not free?"

"Why don't I feel free?"

"Where am I giving my power away?"

"Why am I giving it away to that and why do I feel like it owns me?"

By facing your fears and confusion, the Universe welcomes your contemplative signal, and it begins to send you small sums of money.

Hurray, right?

WRONG.

You feel these amounts are nowhere near enough. You become increasingly frustrated with those small quantities and signal to the Universe, "HEY! What's the deal? This isn't enough money!" and the Universe thinks, "Oh. OK! I'll give you more lack. No problem. I'll keep bringing you more lack! Thanks! Enjoy!"

Before learning the language of the Universe, you can't help but feel confused, frustrated, and angry. You think, "Wait. What am I stating to the Universe? What am I directing to the Universe to bring me? When I feel annoyed, I'm saying, 'bring me MORE of THIS?' Whoa! Back up! That's SO not what I want!"

Here's the hard, cold truth. You must embrace the little bits.

As you're manifesting those little bits, start celebrating them and know that there's no difference, large or small, other than on paper. Energetically there's no difference between a nickel and a hundred dollar bill. As you start celebrating the modest sums and stuffing the bills through the tiny slot on the piggy bank, there's a massive door opening up to manifestation. The amount that's accumulated is just a slight placeholder in your energy field where you're not quite prepared for the more substantial amount that you think you're ready for. Look at that instance as a breather, as if to say, "Ok. If I were ready for this big amount, what would really change? If I received that larger amount, what's my belief around that amount? The larger amount would bring me freedom!" If you believe more money would free you,

you've just moseyed right into a cage and slammed the door behind you.

That means the universe has to keep bringing you ... a cage.

Once you stop believing you're in a cage, then and only then, can you begin to manifest more money.

The cage is very real. If you've got to be free, you're in a cage. If money is the key to your freedom, you'll never be free. You are the key to that freedom. You have the power, but through conditioning or fear, you give your power; you're the keys to your beautiful kingdom to someone or something else. Your strength is your birthright – those keys unlock your unique conscious creation and set you free. When you're liberated, understand that money is just there to show you how willing you are to express your genuine desire and how ready you are to work toward the most authentic expression of what you want.

There are plenty of mental obstacles that can obstruct your road to a prosperous life.

"I'm not smart enough to have 'real money.'"

"What if I make a mistake and end up homeless."

"I'm not married. If it's just me, I'll never have enough money."

"I won't ask for raise because I might rock the boat and lose my job."

"What if I get scammed and lose it all?"

"If I make too much money, people will judge me or think less of me."

"The thought of dealing with money scares me. I don't know what to do or who to trust."

Who are you giving your power to and why are you parting with it?

Are you unsure of your creation?

You can conquer all these fears. It is possible. You are the only person who gets to define who you are. You are the sole proprietor of your own life's work. It's not up to anyone else: your partner, your kids, your priest, your friends, your family, or any financial planner or banker to determine who you are. You're the only one who can write your story.

Our decision to be our most authentic self is what conscious creation is all about. It's about defining and knowing who we are. It's always our choice. The good, the bad and the ugly. It is solely our decision. When we own our power 100% and own it in a divinely inspired way, unabashed and unafraid, we don't run from it, and we sure as hell don't give it away. It is quite literally our "life's work."

As I began to turn my dire financial situation around during that trying time in Los Angeles, I asked myself, "Am I prepared to be the creation of money in my life? Am I ready to step into my power in finances and everywhere else? Am I ready to be the end result – the "Me" being and having everything I'll ever need or want?"

Each day I asked myself that question, "Am I ready?" As I worked to be the keeper of my abundance, my response grew from a weak and wobbly, "I think so?" to a resounding "YES!"

MEDITATION

Right now, I know that I am ready to allow all I AM to receive inspired action, feelings of joy and excitement, and I AM ready to step into my creation in a whole, new way.

I am expression in Action.

I am the abundant flow of the universe.

CHAPTER 21

THE BRAIN

Our brains one of the most amazing gifts we possess, but if there is one complaint I have heard over and over, it is that brains have never come with an instruction manual. It's like giving your grandparent an iPhone 10. They might know how to call a friend and check the time, but there are a hundred more amazing programs running in the background they don't know anything about.

Scientists have recently been able to recreate a virtual brain using a state of the art, multimillion dollar computer. Simulating the electrochemical system we all have in our noggins, they studied how information gets transferred from one place to another. At first the data didn't seem that important. The results were just viewed by what science calls "flat math." The numbers were just numbers and people were beginning to think that it seemed like a waste of time and money.

Then a scientist by the name of Kathryn Hess decided to take a different approach. She used a branch of math called "Algebraic Topology" to look at the data.

"Topology is really the mathematics of connectivity in some sense," Hess says. "It's particularly good at taking local information and integrating it to see what global structures emerge." Where flat math just found basic data, Algebraic Topology looked for the connections. Like the kid's placemat at your favorite restaurant, math found all the numbers, but Algebraic Topology literally connected the dots to see the bigger picture.

Scientists discovered that the eighty-six billion plus neurons in our brains work together in intricate and complex ways. What looked like waves and waves of random firing neurons was actually the brain organizing images into detailed stories and structures. Their study showed that the brain could see objects in as many as eleven dimensions.

Now before you get excited, when they say "dimensions," they're talking about the complexity of shapes. Two neurons connect to make a line. A third one attaches, and the line becomes a triangle. A fourth and the triangle becomes a pyramid. As more and more brain cells joined in the shapes became more and more intricate. Hess described it as though "the human brain is constantly shifting shapes like a sand castle being built and then melting away only to build a new castle." Such a beautiful image for creation.

She also realized that this spatial ability is what gives our brains the power to zoom out. Our brains have the power to look at the leaf. They have the power to pull back further and see the branches to which they are attached. Pull back even further and see the trees themselves. Finally, we see the bigger picture – the forest and the space between it all.

The information Hess worked out from the data was impressive but even more impressive was the process of how she obtained this new information. She took the flat math and expanded it to see it from another angle. A new dimension of itself. Just like the brain, she pulled back to see the bigger picture which was the dimension surrounding the flat math. The next level.

What always excites me about stories like this is looking back at how far we have come in science and the amazing advances we have made but even more exciting how many more "next levels" there are ahead of us.

We are getting better and better at understanding the "how" of the human brain. It almost parallels the invention of computers. First, we discovered the past the basic gears and switches. Baby steps like Descartes' "I think therefore I am." When we discovered brain cells and mapped neural pathways, we figured out we used an energy source and wiring and vacuum tubes. Right now we are only beginning to understand the brain's remarkable potential. The next steps will be like inventing processors and microchips with faster ways to process information. We'll discover the next level on how the computer connects to other computers like Bluetooth and the Internet. Exploring all the different ways the computer can create and make our everyday lives better. We're always upgrading to the most sophisticated technology.

The one major difference is that we aren't creating the technology of the human brain. We are just trying to understand it. We are trying to reverse engineer it.

Each of us already owns the most sophisticated piece of technology. We ARE this supercomputer. The next level, the step back to see the forest, is understanding the "whole brain." Not just how all the parts work but the synergy of how they work together. Our brain doesn't just have an electromagnetic field, but that field is actually us. We are the electromagnetic frequency.

The physical brain interprets the light of who we are as it is brought into physical form. WE have the power to shape that energy through creating new dimensional pictures through our thoughts, actions, and most importantly, our feelings.

Feelings are the gasoline in the engine of manifestation. Simply put, they are a large part of the missing instruction manual and by understanding how to alter and choose how we feel; we learn how to take the reins and operate our new device!

We have sophisticated programming running in the background at all times. The Ego that allows us to individuate ourselves and the (not so helpful) Alter Ego that sometimes makes our programs crash. We connect and communicate with through universal energy that is all around us. You can call it Source or Spirit or God, but it is a pure energy we can tap into at any time-even without a password.

And as for creating and making life better? Our computer shapes our world. It is our life and is so multi-dimensional and timeless that it actually created itself.

Without the instruction manual and this awareness, many people live their whole life never aware of how powerful their computer really is.

They are focused on the leaves and don't see the forest.

They are the grandparents with an iPhone 10. Just using it to check the time.

MEDITATION

What does completion feel like?

How am I defining it?

What do I need to be or do or have, in my mind, in order to feel complete?

Through utilizing my new operating system, I am choosing to open the app of allowance.

So, how would I feel if I were complete?

Right now, I am going to let go of any stories about who I have to be, or what I might have to do, and I am going to play.

I am going to play with how it feels to be complete.

CHAPTER 22

GRIEF & PAIN

One of the hardest and sadly most inevitable challenges we will face in life is the loss of a loved one. Whether it's an illness than lingers over time, or a quick death that happens in a heartbeat, the moment will come when you're suddenly in a space where your mother, grandfather, your best friend, your beloved family pet, are gone.

Just like that, it's over.

The stark realization of loss tears us away from the moment of now. Half of our brain is remembering all of the wonderful past we shared with them and the other half of our brain is frozen in panic of what the future will look like without them. We forget that we are still living, still breathing, and still have to live in the now.

Grief, for many of us in this position, is inevitable, because we feel the loss as something permanent. Even if we know we will see them again someday, not having them present, now, seems like a shock and an insurmountable mountain of emotion to overcome.

As such, grief can be especially hard to grasp and move through in today's world. We live in a globalized space of advanced technological wonders. We can communicate with anyone anywhere. Less than one hundred years ago if someone you knew moved to another country, other than written correspondence, that may be the last time you ever saw or heard from them again. But, we now live in an age where you can board a plane, fly anywhere in the world, and feel your loved ones safe in your arms in a matter of hours. With the simple tap of a few computer buttons you can see and hear your wife, your business partner, your children, even if they are on the other side of the planet. So to suddenly lose someone and feel as if you will never be able to communicate with them again can devastate you and bring you to your knees.

That's what our grief is. We grieve because we want that channel of communication to be open again if even just for a second. We think of our loved ones – and ourselves – as being finite and existing only on this one plane. When the reality is our connection to them and our relationship with them has been energy since the moment we met. We rely on our five (or more) senses and think that a person is made up of what we miss most about them when they're gone. We cry because we will never see their smile again or get a big warm hug from them. We will never hear their laugh or smell their cologne or perfume. We hold onto these things dearly. But those are all physical things from the physical plane.

A relationship between two people is based on the energy we receive from them and the energy they receive from us. It is a shared experience between two eternal beings. In that way, grieving is almost like a state of confusion. It's a paradox where our brain is saying that door has closed forever while another part of us – the deeper part of us who knows who we truly are as infinite *Source* – knows that the energy is and always will continue to be shared and received: the love, the laughs, the sorrow and joy – it all exists in the energy we breathe, the energy which nourishes through our thoughts and feelings, and the energy we feel as we create ourselves anew in every moment.

There's no other way to say it. Grief sucks. It's as if confusion and torture had a baby and you got stuck with permanent babysitting duty. But the thing is, when you can tap into the essence of what you're grieving, understand the loss and incorporate the knowing that we are all connected as we are all One energy, that grief can fade, step by step, into a celebration of that person, place, or thing, around which you'd previously felt immense pain and sorrow. And that celebration begins to do an interesting thing: it re-awakens your connection. It opens your heart, and suddenly, you feel connected once more.

No two people deal with grief the same way, nor should they. When some people see grief coming they try to busy themselves or bury themselves in work, hobbies, addictions, or even drama to push away the feelings. They think if they occupy their conscious mind with work or a sudden need to clean the house from top to bottom, they can escape it; that it somehow won't find them and it will just ease on down the road. Or, we decide to turn to worldly things which we think – possibly at the subconscious level – will void ourselves completely, so we can feel nothing about anything at all: If we go numb to everything we won't feel the grief.

We are complex creatures capable of both thoughts and feelings and when things hurt, our natural tendency is to dive in and never come back, shut down completely, or find a middle ground. Whatever we do, we usually do because we don't want to feel the grief. But the thing about not feeling the feeling is that whatever we avoid through resistance grows and grows until it gets out of control and manifests in more destructive ways.

Many people familiar with energy acknowledge that avoiding grief is resisting it and that acceptance is the key to really allowing the release and creating a new space. However, acceptance alone doesn't lead to change. If you're being poked by a sharp stick over and over again, it's hard to sit there and accept that you're going to be poked repeatedly with a sharp stick. Acceptance has no purpose if it does not include action.

When we advocate to "accept pain" we don't mean to enjoy it like the Marquis De Sade, but rather, to use pain as a multidimensional tool. In order to do so, we need to understand what pain is.

The Buddha famously said, "All life is pain." This sounds incredibly depressing and makes the Buddha seem like the last person you'd want to invite to your birthday party. But he was right. Pain is a very important part of life.

Psychologically, as people, we have a need to anthropomorphize things. We like to give inanimate objects human traits and motives. For example, that time you tried to feed your crumpled dollar bill to a vending machine that spit it out again and again. At best, you felt like it might be a picky eater who didn't like the taste of your money and at worst that damn machine KNEW you only had two minutes left on your lunch break and was purposely teasing you by not giving you your Dark Chocolate Milky Way bar, (the latter is why more people are killed by vending machines than sharks every year).

If there's one thing we all like to anthropomorphize, its pain. We tend to think of it as a synonym for suffering and torture. We like to think it take's joy in hurting us. That there is some pleasure to be had for our feeling pain. But really, just like the vending machine, it's simply doing its job.

Without physical pain we would never have survived as a species. Our entire body, every piece, is wired with a nervous system that's sole job is to send signals to our brain to let us know we are in pain. Whether it's the tooth with a cavity at the back of our mouth, the stinging bee we just sat down on, or our little toe landing on Lego piece our kid left on the floor, our body screams a message at lightning speed, sending us waves of debilitating pain. And, thank God it does. That's its job to let us know we're injured and those injuries could be life threatening. We could train our minds to shut off these signals or learn to live with agonizing pain. But, we don't. We do something about it. We see a doctor. We teach our kids to clean up their toys. We acknowledge the pain and we do something about it. We think of pain as something to hurt us, but it is simply trying to point out that something's wrong. The smoke detector isn't trying to ruin your dinner when you burn the steak and the alarm clock (which YOU set) is not gleefully trying to wreck a good night's sleep. It's a sudden and jolting shock that is trying to get you to do something. It is a call to action. And Pain is one way we experience the contrast in our lives, which shows us, "Hey, this is not where you want to be. You were not made for this! You have a much bigger purpose, and it is time to act!"

If you are being poked with that stick, you can ignore the pain, resist and pretend it doesn't hurt…but it does. You can accept the pain. Stop resisting and just accept you will be stabbed again and again. You will dwell on it. On how sharp that point is and how many times you are being hit. On how unfair it is. But this is focusing on the action of being poked. You need to acknowledge that pain, but more you need to figure out the reason that stick is poking you in the first place. Underneath your experience you need to realize what your call to action really is. It might be you aren't in the right place. Maybe the stick is trying to get you to move over. And by moving over, you it's saving your life.

Emotional pain is no different. It's important to acknowledge it as a warning call letting you know that your life is in a crisis. You are about to face huge change. Feel that pain. Acknowledge that pain but please, please, please, never look for blame for the pain. So many times we feel there is a karmic reason why we are going through great loss. We want to have someone to blame for such a tragedy and especially blame ourselves. This is not about pay back for something 18 past lives ago. This is not for not thinking enough happy thoughts. You aren't being punished for not throwing some change in that homeless person's coffee cup. This is just the energy of the universe unfolding through us in a physical experience and by giving ourselves a small space to say "Hey. This is happening. This is painful and I do miss my partner. I do miss my parent, my friend, my child, or my puppy, Parker" we are actually open a door to healing.

Every call to action is different. Unique to every person and every person's situation. When we find ourselves in pain we can work out why we hurt and take back our power. We can focus on our own energy by choosing how to move forward. When we feel the pain of a cold empty house it might mean looking for our new place of warmth. If it is the unbearable irony of having lost that one person we would share this pain with, the call to action might be finding someone else we can be vulnerable with. If it is just the grief of not being able to see their smile or the shock of hearing their voice on an old answering machine message or the smell of their sweater, when you really just really miss them it might be as simple as releasing the physical memories of them and receiving the energies that they have, still do, and always will be sending you.

Healing will take time. I know this sounds like an oxymoron but it takes a long time to make a sudden change. What I've found is that a lot of times we heal in small immeasurable ways. A lot of small changes at a time that we aren't even aware of. Then suddenly one day we realize we are healed.

All life is pain, not because life sucks, but because life is really all choice. And for eons of time, through duality, humanity has used pain – or contrast – as a means to create. But what if we could change that?

By stepping into our hearts, by opening and expanding to the reality that All are One, and that we are in turn, infinite... by understanding the nature of life as choice and experience and that WE have the power to create through our feelings, our thoughts, and our actions, we realize life is not in fact pain, but life is choice.

Life is a call to action. And today, as best as you can, what if that action was to love yourself as *Source* loves you: no story, no blame or shame, simply love?

MEDITATION:

Source, you know that sometimes in my life, I feel contrast. I feel grief. Give me an understanding of what this represents and a willing spirit to commit to knowing what I know, and knowing who I AM:

I Am Infinite.

I Am Connected.

I Am the open heart of joy, ever expanding and choosing, and right now, I choose Love.

I choose Union.

I choose Connection.

And so it is.

CHAPTER 23

LETTING GO OF CLUTTER

*My brain is so filled with random thoughts, regrets, fears
and worries and I can't sleep at night.*

*There's so much clutter in my house that
I feel trapped and ashamed.*

*I've been holding on to so many theories, beliefs and old
ideas that I don't know what to believe anymore.*

*I can't relax and enjoy anything while I'm hemmed
in by stuff. I'm overwhelmed with anxiety because it's
distracting and it makes me feel like a failure.*

In our modern day world, it appears we are no longer embracing the saying, "Out with the old, and in with the new." We're bringing in tons of the new but keeping the old for a whole host of reasons: We might need it, we love (or loved) it and can't part with it, we are afraid we may not be able to create it again, or having things around makes us feel safe and satiated; that is until the next shiny object or obsessive thought makes its way into our psyche. While we're trying to fill a hole inside us either mentally or physically, our accumulating "fixes" are suffocating us.

Clutter is not just random French bulldog tchotchkes and piles of unworn workout clothes. Clutter is an outward reflection of our inner world. Sometimes our inner world is cluttered with old paradigms, worn out belief systems, and negative thoughts that no longer serve us. The mental static can be so thick that we're unable to feel or see our way into who we are, who we've truly become or who we've evolved into. This clutter manifests in the outer world in myriad ways, such as mountains of magazines, bills or an army of vitamin bottles on your kitchen counter, or an office desk that resembles a recently detonated bombsite.

Our issues with clutter are a sign of a more significant problem.

But what exactly *is* the problem?

There are numerous reasons we keep our mental and physical clutter around us. Sometimes it's to abdicate the responsibilities of the adult world. "If I hide those bills I can't pay in a box, I won't have to deal with them for a while." Out of sight, out of mind.

Sometimes our clutter is personal and seemingly serves a purpose for us. You may have a two-foot-high stack of your grandma's favorite Maeve Binchy novels taking up space in your bookcase, but you don't have the heart to throw them out. A second winter coat you bought in 2002 that doesn't fit and was worn only once might be needed in case of an emergency. You have your dad's old hunting rifle nestled in your hall closet. It no longer fires, but it makes you feel secure at night. We think we need these things to remind us of people we've lost, have a backup in case we lose everything, and hold on to something to make us feel less afraid. But things are not the answer, no matter how much we acquire and how tightly we hang on to them.

The other clutter we cling to is painful, destructive thoughts, feelings, beliefs and negative memories that have been hanging around for decades. Releasing these heavy vibrations may help you move through past emotional barriers and embrace a higher awareness. They're telling you to forgive and let go completely, cleansing and clearing your mind, body, and spirit. Rejuvenating all that you truly are. When you release these places, you're freeing the awareness. These barriers are useless. You will not need them in the future because they no longer serve you. Let them go and allow your heart to open up to giving and receiving fully. You don't need to hold on to anything. When you let go of what you're clinging to, you receive what you really need. What you need and what you're truly asking for is the experience and expansion of receiving it all.

Know at the deepest level that you are held safe and secure by all that is. In fact, there's no need for safety because beyond the polarity of "safe" and "unsafe" exists the truth of who you truly are; the creation of all that is. You can accumulate a mountain of things to pad the walls you've built around yourself, but your authentic self is always your best security system.

Allow the frequencies and the energy of love to build within you, stimulating a sense of harmony and balance in the body and helping it release any anger, frustration or memory trauma from the cells to bring about more peace and emotional wellbeing within your mind and the body. Let go of the negative emotions and frustration and open up to the love, joy and freedom that allow you to navigate a path free from clutter.

So often we hold on so tightly to what we think is ours, to what we think we need, what we think we need to create, to what we think will "get us there." But the Universe is asking us to open up and let go. Allow yourself to let go. Allow yourself to move into the energy of the blank page, of the still point. Allow your mind to declutter. Allow for regeneration and renewal. Make room for new neural pathways to form. Direct yourself to open new channels of information but also new channels of experience, of money, of knowing that by releasing whatever's cluttering your life, you are opening up to understanding that in every single moment you have what you need. You can create whatever you need. You don't need to hold on to anything. You always have what you need or you can create what you need.

Clear your path. Establish new networks and new thought processes. Let new possibilities and potentials flood your environment, your mind and your body. Remove the clutter that's been holding you back, that's been stagnating your brain and engulfing you in a life that obstructed your brilliant light.

MEDITATION

Clear the path to abundance, joy and love.

Unlock the spaces and places in you that long to be unleashed.

Let go of all that doesn't serve you, so what is yet to come can pour in. Release the old and open up to a new experience of you.

"I know that I am abundant and loved. I know the universe always provides for me and I allow myself to clear a space to truly know myself and my new space, so I can make it whatever I choose."

CHAPTER 24

THE BEST

L et me tell you a story about a man named John. John had spent his entire life dreaming of running in a 10K race. He trained for months and months, barely taking time for anything else. Every day he did the work he knew he needed to do in order to make his goals of not only running in, but also winning this race, reality.

After nearly two years of hard work and dedication, the big day finally arrived. John got out onto that street and when the starting line marker went off, he took off like the wind. John pushed himself harder than he ever had before and could feel himself becoming drained as he watched the kilometers tick by. On the final lap, in the home stretch, John turned a corner, where he saw it: the big, bright red ribbon of the finish line.

John *knew* he could make it.

In that moment, John crossed the finish line and went from having a dream, to making the dream a reality. Yet something

138 | THE *Answer* IS *Energy*

didn't feel right.

In the days that followed, John found himself depressed. He realized that he had not been ready for the race to truly over. John had become addicted to the preparation, the training, the buildup and the want, and now, he felt like a man without a dream.

Like the dog that caught the car, John suddenly found himself in a weird position: what now?

We've all had those so-called runners high in life, where we feel value and worth as we pursue a goal. Yet, with that high, we often find ourselves experiencing tremendous lows, because without that pursuit, who and what are we? What's the purpose?

The story of John is a basic explanation of why so many of us stay in an energy and vibration of "want" as opposed to "have." Our bodies become dependent on the ride of healing, working, building, etc., and thus, we create an ever expanding loop of never quite getting there, because in getting there, we have to shift our stories and identities. When we get "there," if we finish that race, if we get that relationship, then what? We fear we have to move on to the next thing, or that we won't even know what the next thing is, and so, we begin shutting down. Subject by subject, we start creating ways of spinning our wheels and we stay in the energy of want, because even though it may be uncomfortable, it is familiar.

We unwittingly become like Sisyphus, who was cursed to roll a boulder up hill, only for the boulder to always fall back to the bottom just as it reached the top. We energetically become attached to "almost" as our definition of whole. We roll our boulders of relationships, career, finance and self-worth right up that hill, and just as we get to the top, we let it slide and roll back down to the bottom again.

There are a myriad of reasons for this slide and repeat. At times you may simply be overwhelmed with your creation. You may feel as if you just don't have the energy to continue. Or, maybe once you begin tapping into the energies around you and seeing how limitless your possibilities are, you simply become intimidated or stuck. Maybe there is a belief that you're only allowed to get close to what you want but never allowed to "seal the deal" because once you do, you're never going to get anything ever again. "I can only create once." Or "I better get it right, because this is my only chance!" It's an Aladdin mentality where you are allowed only one wish and you can't wish for more wishes, so you'd better make this one count. Suddenly you're afraid to "pull the trigger."

In the theatre, they always say, "If you introduce a gun in the first act of a play, it has to be used in the last." When we ask the universe what we want, it is like we are introducing that gun. We know we have asked for something to happen. We work and work toward opening ourselves up and making progress, but when we start to get closer to achieving that vibration or tuning into that frequency, we waver. We hesitate. If we "pull the trigger" and get what we want, it means the show will be over. It will go away. The end. So we think "I better save it for when I *want* it to be over." You're seeing the world as finite, when in fact, it is infinite. You can create… and create… and then create some more.

This isn't the end of your play. This might be the end of your first act- but it is the first of many acts to come. By pulling that trigger, you can see what comes next. You can set your sights on even bigger targets. There will always be another goal, and now you have the tools to see exactly what that goal may be.

You may also find yourself butting up against another common belief: If I create what I want, someone or something will take it from me." So, in order to save yourself the feelings of loss, you choose to simply never create what you want. What if no matter what, you knew you were sovereign and loved, safe to create anything, whenever you desired? Would you then commit to the race?

Sometimes we quit the race because we are too short sighted and don't confront the real issue. We want change instantaneously: the new house, the perfect relationship, the new job. We see the world as cause and effect. We look at the effect and say, "I don't like this pain in my shoulder/big bills/relationship problem," so we enlist our ego to solve the problem because heck, its main job is to problem solve. The ego comes up with a quick solution and the problem goes away... for a while. But that's the shortcoming of the ego. It never really sees the big picture. It has put a temporary fix on the problem, usually solving it *enough* so we can get back to doing what is causing the trouble in the first place.

Self: My leg hurts.

Ego: Okay, quit the race.

Self: This relationship is uncomfortable.

Ego: Okay, dump the relationship or shut yourself off emotionally!

The ego problem solves in a way which may provide some form of relief, but it is not always the real relief you are seeking. You may be focusing so much on what you don't want (and not on what you actually want, i.e. to feel loved, to feel whole, to cross that finish line and come full circle in creation), that you wind up tossing it all out the window, only to find yourself right back in the same life pattern down the road.

When we do this, we are focus on the effect and ignoring the real cause.

How many times have you said, "I want to lose weight? I am

going to lose weight!" You force down plates of health food that you don't really enjoy. You deny yourself the candy and treats. You work out on a treadmill for hours, and you start to see changes. You are doing it! Then, one day, it falls apart. You have a slice of cake... or two... or three. You order whatever you want at the business dinner you couldn't get out of, and suddenly, there goes Sisyphus chasing after the boulder.

What you had focused on was the effect and not the cause. You wanted to lose weight. You focused on that aspect and the energy of what you wanted to resist or push away, and in doing so, you locked yourself into a system of duality with right ways and wrong ways and you limited yourself. When you open the heart, you begin to realize that it isn't about the effect, it's about the cause, and the cause is something deeper within. It might be the reason why you fill yourself with food. The only energy you feel you're connected to is food. Or maybe it's the physical replacement for the nourishment you are spiritually missing in your life. Denying yourself what you wanted was putting all your energy into what you need to keep away. Instead, you need to open up and find what it was you needed to allow *in* like finding a love of foods that are healthy or discovering the joy of going for a walk with a friend. Maybe it's renting skates and going ice-skating. It isn't about trying to become a new person; it's about discovering the person you actually are at source. In doing so, you also ease up on yourself, and can say, "Okay, today, I wasn't able to focus on what I wanted. I became vulnerable and I created a lack of what I would allow, which caused me to want it more and I gave in. Instead of beating myself up, I am going to love myself and I am going to accept who I am right now, let go of the resistance to my body, and go about creating it in a fun and joyful way, beginning now.

It's possible that you can't move through your struggle because you've chosen to believe, at some level of consciousness, that you aren't ready for it. This is that subconscious space where you feel there's always something more exciting about the chasing than the catching. You may have thought your entire life that you would like to have money, and felt like you've begged the universe for just that. But once you have money, who are you then? Do you have the ability to hold that energy of wealth? A lot of lottery winners wind up going broke only a few years after winning. They were capable of allowing in that massive amount of energy, but they were unable to hold it. Again, like the dog that caught the car, they simply didn't know what to do with it once they got it.

We don't just do this with physical creation, either. We sometimes purposely stay separate from source and feelings of oneness and love. We don't want to cross that next level of vibration because we fear it will take away our individuality. In a way, we sometimes feel special by giving ourselves stories of struggle. I know this sounds strange, and if you ever dared to say to someone laid up in a hospital bed that they should "enjoy their struggle," I am sure you would have something thrown at your head, but we define ourselves by what we are fighting. We want to stay who we are... just change. And that is a paradox. Who we are, is why we have created the space we are in. To create a new space, we have to change who we are and what we will allow.

Often times, we stare down at the puzzle pieces the universe has given us over the course of our lives, and we say, "I just need that ONE perfect piece to get this all together.

The universe starts dropping off pieces, and we get so frustrated because none of those pieces fit our puzzle. The thing is, the universe is showing us, "it's time to do a different puzzle." It's time to be a new creation. That old puzzle is old. It is not you anymore.

It isn't who you really are. But, we let our fear of change, and fear of an unsecure future rule our thoughts, and thus, we keep tossing those new pieces in the trash, demanding and knowing that the universe will eventually send us "the right damn piece!"

When we allow ourselves to go deeper, look deeper and really consciously look at who we are, and why we are that way, through the lens of divine love, we open further to pure truth. Not just the pure truth of situations but the pure truth of ourselves. There are parts of us that are afraid we're going to be left behind. We sometimes stop ourselves from moving on into higher vibration, feelings and experiences because, whether it's a part of our inner child, our subconscious or just simply something floating in our energy field that we may not even know about, there is some part of us we don't want to leave behind. So, we stay with that part and we love that part and feel we are nurturing it, but what we are really doing is holding ourselves back by buying into our own excuses and forgetting that we govern our own lives.

In all of these scenarios, the constants are fear and limitation. It's us either clinging to what we were or what we might become. What we are forgetting is what we *are*. At the *Source* self, we *are* all of these things. The past, present *and* the future are all part of you. And, you get to take the parts that you love into the next moment. You get to choose what continues and what you release, in love, because you are always whole. So, how do you define that whole?

You do not have to settle.

You can do better than just "good enough." If you choose to.

Don't let your stories stop you short.

Instead, change them. Let them go. Redefine and re-choose.

Cross the finish line and be the best you, in every single moment. Because that moment will create the next… and the next… and the next.

MEDITATION

Right now, I choose to accept myself. I know that, just like in building a house, I may come to a space where my hands are weary or my legs are tired, and yet I know that my goals are accomplishable. I know that it is okay to allow myself to be in a body and experience who I am, while I also know and acknowledge that I get to steer this ship and create who and what I am.

Right now, I commit to loving myself in every way possible, while constantly expanding upon those same possibilities.

I commit to being the best me I can possibly be, in every moment, loving myself each step of the way, because I was created of pure love. And even though I may have forgotten this in the past, I know it and take it into my heart right now, that I may know I am always enough, always worthy, and always loved.

I am that I am.

And so it is.

CHAPTER 25

THE SOUNDTRACK OF OUR LIVES

"Music hath charms to soothe a savage breast, to soften rocks, or bend a knotted oak."

While this is a line from an exquisite poem by William Congreve, you have probably heard the more popular paraphrasing, "Music hath charms to soothe a savage *beast*." No, you aren't experiencing a Mandela Effect. Back in the 1950's people were too embarrassed to say "savage *breast*," but in editing it, the revisionists were missing what Congreve was actually saying. When he said "breast," he wasn't rude or tawdry. He merely meant "chest" or more specifically – "the heart."

William Congreve was writing about the power of music to transform those around us. He was trying to influence the very physics of the world and to sway even the angriest person's heart from rage to love. He believed in the power of music. He believed we hear music not with the mind or the ear, but it is energy we hear first with our hearts.

Even without words, music can instill great emotions in us. There's a reason Hollywood employs only the best composers to underscore their movies with it and leave profound, sometimes lifelong effects on the audience. Think about it. Two musical notes from the movie "Jaws" instill instant panic in viewers to this day. Music appeals not to our conscious brains but to that part of the whole brain that feels rather than thinks. Whether it's a love scene or a car chase, music heightens what we feel and puts us right in the scene with the actors.

There are very few things that religions around the world can agree on, but every single last one of them includes music as a component of their rituals. From Native American drum circles to explosive Baptist Gospel singers or Tuvan throat singing, from Jewish Cantors to Gregorian Chanters; they all understand there is a purer energy we tap into when we combine faith with music.

Our oldest mythologies not only talk about sound and its connection to faith but that was an actual way to pass history down through the generations. John 1:1 begins with "In the beginning, there was the word. And the word was God. The word given to us."

That is the language of light. Sound made manifest. The words we say.

When Zen Buddhists asked their master Dōgen whether their prayers (or sutra) should be chanted or humbly read, he said: "Painted rice cakes cannot satisfy hunger." In other words, a prayer is not meant to be a representation or a symbol, but to be experienced by all the senses. Taken in through the eye and the nose and the mouth and absorbed by the body. You need to become the prayer.

When we sing or chant, we are infusing our energy back and tuning ourselves to harmonize with the energy we are receiving from the universe. We aren't only reading it and saying, "Ok. Got it! Let's move on." We are responding and having a conversation with the universe in our frequency – our own individuated vibration.

Scientifically, that is what all sounds are – vibrations. Ancient Greece philosopher Pythagoras is credited with this discovery. You might remember the name from math class. He was the A squared plus B squared equals C squared guy. That was his triangle. Pythagoras saw everything through math. It was his way of tapping into the energy of the universe.

One day, while walking through the Agora, Pythagoras noticed the clanging of hammers at the blacksmith shops and the sound they made stuck in his ears. Sometimes they seemed to harmonize and match perfectly (assonance) and sometimes the notes clashed horribly (dissonance). He ran into the shops to study the hammers and realized it all had to do with the size. A hammer exactly half the size of another made a sound that matched (an octave higher); whereas a hammer that is 1/3 the size might clash. They vibrated when struck and the size of the hammer made different vibrations.

Pythagoras also noticed the same thing when he played his lyre. The vibration of the string caused the sound, and the length of the chord affected the pitch of the sound. By playing with which notes seemed to be assonant and which are dissonant, he discovered the seven notes that make up one octave. He *translated* music. The universe spoke to him through mathematics and he realized there was music to everything around him. He began to see it in nature and everyday objects, realizing it must be in the movement of the planets and even in the human soul itself. He believed everything was energy and what's more, they can all be harmonized- creating what he called the "Music of the Spheres."

The philosopher believed each of the planets must have their own signature frequency, and if we could attune ourselves to those frequencies, we might be able to use the energy to heal and to speak with the cosmos. He named this "eurhythmics." And no. He never started a band with Annie Lennox. "Eurhythmics" simply means to be "in rhythm or to attain harmonious order."

On a purely instinctual level, we can sense harmony. We crave it. We know when we are joining the chorus and when we are off key.

My own experience as a kid was to be off tempo. I had a heart condition where my heart was off beat. I literally was arrhythmic. There is no coincidence that I also had feelings that I didn't belong. My life was out of key and I wasn't in tempo with the world around me. I was trying to match everyone else's frequency and that wasn't me. They were all playing polka, and I was playing a sonata. I needed to discover my own music.

Too often, we don't stop to listen close enough to the soundtrack we have in our own life. There is a symphony inside us that we are broadcasting to the universe. Every aspect of our life is a delicate piece of our orchestra. Money might be the string section. Relationships may be percussion. Family could be your horn section or harps. They all need to be in harmony, and one note from one section might be dissonant from another section. Sometimes it's hard to pinpoint what instrument is out of tune but believe me; you can hear that it's off.

Through our understanding of frequency, we can get ourselves in tune. Frequencies are just belief systems. Every single thought that we have has a resonant vibration and frequency.

The Creation Formula is like a map of non-dimensional time and space, tuning the wavelengths of which you are at *Source* energy and allowing it to expand. The key is finding the sheet music to your soundtrack.

I often help to center people that are in panic mode. Nothing seems to be right and their orchestra sounds like a bunch of monkeys slamming symbols together. One of the first things I ask them to do is to close their eyes, take a deep breath and exhale with a sound. That sound is the most essential part of the equation. Sound is the energy of the universe made manifest in the matter and space of our body. You take air into our lungs, and then through the breathing out, you feel the vibrations of our vocal chords. We are tuning into our Source energy and allowing that power to come into our airspace. By releasing our sound back into the Source, we are harmonizing with the universe.

Pythagoras lived over 2500 years ago and based his ideas on the hammering of blacksmiths. Today, in the age of subatomic microscopes, they are studying a new theory called Superstring theory. Scientists are trying to discover if the smallest part of the atom, the electron, might be made up of an even *smaller* particle – a tiny string. Like a violin string. They believe the energy of all matter might come from its vibration and that different frequencies result in the various matters it creates.

Music *may* be able to change the very physics of the world around us. By honoring and tuning our own energy, we can affect the world as well. We can bring peace and change to others and ourselves by aligning and optimizing our energetic instruments with love.

I believe Pythagoras would agree. Sweet dreams are made of these.

MEDITATION

Take in a breath and exhale, connecting with sound. Allow yourself to really feel the sound as you connect into your body. So often, as energy workers, we want to be "out there," yet our true power is being fully integrated.

I allow myself the space and freedom of my own body.

I allow my song to be sung.

I am the beautiful symphony of all that I AM being made manifest in my life, right now.

CHAPTER 26

ABUNDANCE

Whenever we feel trapped in life, especially in the areas of finance and relationships, we can feel like we are stuck in a room with no doors, and the walls consistently feel like they are closing in. It feels tight and it feels uncomfortable. Ultimately, we feel a lack – whether it is a lack of safety, love, comfort, money, or freedom. Our thoughts can easily begin moving down the road of "I see others living abundant lives. Why doesn't abundance show up for me? Why can't I have what I want? Why is it SO hard?" Strangely, the answer to these questions of abundance and wholeness doesn't exist within wanting it more, visualizing it more, even in pushing it more. We often think, "If I can just grab that brass ring of abundance, everything would change." But what if the true answer was in letting go?

The broadest, most complete and whole definition of true abundance is freedom. True feeling is our ability to feel and know we are supported in all things; it is the ability to express whatever it is we are here to express. In that sense, freedom is all about the capacity to express exactly who we are in the most authentic, abundant, and divine, natural way.

When I say, "natural way," I mean who we are beyond our stories of who we think we're supposed to be, who we think we should have been, or who we think we should actually be. We may have done some things that we perceptually see as taking wrong turns, or perhaps we don't understand why we're in the place we're in right now, and we're not seeing the gifts that are available to us. I know I've certainly thought that way. At a certain time if someone had said to me, "Hey! This moment is a gift." I would have replied, "Well, is there a receipt in the bag? Because I don't want it!"

As strange as it sounds, letting go of "want" energy actually aligns you with "what is," and as uncomfortable as "what is" can be sometimes, acceptance allows resistance to fall away, which then allows us to free massive amounts of energy. We can then direct that energy into creating what we desire, instead of broadcasting a signal of lack or want. In that way, the freedom of abundance is a multi-leveled process where we're able to come to the place where we don't feel resistance to life. We go from re-action, to action. We see clearly that we are the captains of our own ship.

Many people automatically think abundance is just about money. While abundance *is* that, it's also so much *more* than that. I often see among light workers and energy healers a separation between the energies of "abundance" and "money." It's not anything conscious – because everyone would like to have monetary freedom – but there's a separation that says, "To be whole (and thus have money), I have to be well first" or "Money is not Spiritual, and true Abundance is Love." It's like they've formed a mental triangle of relationships, health and money. They believe, "Well, I've got to have money to have the relationship, and I have to have health to have the relationship, and I've got to have the relationship to have this..." But I also have to be spiritual. It's like a gigantic DNA helix of collapsed belief systems about what we have to do to have that freedom. And the truth is, we have become so used to "either/or" dynamics, that we often forget we can replace "this or that" with "this AND that." We CAN have it all. It just takes some restructuring within our self-defined programming.

There are so many great Zen adages and proverbs about attachment and being attached to things. So many times we think if we lose the attachment to something we want, we won't get it. We think, "I really want *this*. But if I let go of the wanting of it, how am I supposed to get it?" We've been trained to hold our focus on want, and want becomes the vibration we hold. But really that's the vibration, on a whole host of levels, which puts the brakes on and says, "Whoa. Hold up." It's the idea of "what you resist persists," but it's the same way with attachment. The Universe is simply a vibrational "call and answer," and when we have the desire of want, the universe just says, "Okay, send more want!"

I once heard a wise man put it this way, "If you had not eaten in days, would you rather want a meal... or HAVE it?" Vibrationally, there is a massive difference. When we allow the want to go by moving into the playing of what it would feel like to have, we begin to change our resonance and open to receiving in a new way, but to do this, we often come face to face with the biggest "A" there is – attachment!

Many times attachment is just the flip side of resistance. There's an attachment to getting something, because we believe having it will help get us OUT of what we have currently created. I often see this with health, but I also see it with money as well. For instance, "I have to have this job to pay my bills and get out of debt," or "I want to be healthy... but not because I love and celebrate myself and my expression, but because I DON'T want to be sick." It could be and is often for a very valid reason. "I need to work so I can feed my family. I need to work so I can pay my bills." I myself have been in those places, as well.

But there is a place where we can tune in to our own I AM presence – that space of balance and peace, which resides in, with and as all of us, where we can begin to feel whole right now. And, in this wholeness, we open to new thoughts, new inspirations... it's as if that small room with no windows or doors suddenly has one door, then two, then windows and the room even begins to expand. Sometimes, the roof blows off and we elevate into a whole new perspective and space! And as we do this, as we let go of resisting what is and begin to consciously attune ourselves to what it feels like to have, while also consciously acting on inspiration, our "problems" begin to decrease and become smaller and smaller and smaller. Until suddenly, the resistance or attachment to solving or releasing those issues goes away. What was once a problem is now viewed in hindsight as a huge opportunity for us to step into a new awareness, wherein we can vibrationally and physically hold the very energies we spent so many years "wanting" in the first place.

In that space, we find the freedom to birth something new and embark on our own journey of pure creation and *true* abundance. This space is the freedom that allows us the true definition of abundance, because we are no longer broadcasting a lack or victim story from the ego, but rather we become centered in our hearts and begin to feel a new found peace and knowing – which then shifts our vibration into a whole new space, allowing us to create and live in that space. In that freedom there *is* abundance. There is physical abundance, spiritual abundance and all the love in the world we can tap into and feel. We always have enough.

I was having a conversation with a friend recently about the word "enough" and what "enough" meant. We were discussing how there are certain ways we say that word. Sometimes enough means, "Stop! That's enough. I don't want any more." Sometimes we use that word when we think or talk about abundance, we often say, "I just need enough."

If we can begin to reframe the word "enough" where it doesn't mean, "I just need enough to pay my bills" but "I always *have* enough" we shift the message to, "Ok. I have enough to pay my bills. What does that mean? It means I have enough and after that, I have enough because I have so much left over and there's always enough – no matter what I am choosing to create. If I have enough to pay my bills and there's always enough, and I want to do something else, I have enough for that, too." The hyperbolic example for that would be, "I have enough to pay my bills, and I'd like to have enough to go to dinner. And I'd like to go to dinner in a new car. Guess what? I have enough for a new car, and I want to take that new car on vacation. Hey! I have enough for that vacation."

Can you feel that? Or do you feel resistance to that? What if you just decided, right now, to let the resistance be what it is and focus on how it would feel – not what you have to do, or be, or have, but simply feel into the bounty of "enough?"

The Universe is always flowing. The current is always there and the river is always wide and full. Yet, for a very long time, abundance – particularly with regards to money – was energy of "stockpiling." It was all about control, whether of self or other. The stockpile energy is the energy of scarcity, and as we collectively move into a wider and higher vibration, that old energy is no longer supported. Money, and indeed abundance in all subjects, is truly energy of expression – how willing we are to be seen, and in turn see ourselves. You can have all the monetary things you desire, the key is, as the proverb goes, not to let them have you.

Lots of times, we think, "Well, if I just had this much in the bank, I'd be safe." In that regard, we are really saying "I don't know I create until I have it," and the Universe replies, "Okay; send more "I don't know!" That contrast is not a punishment; it is merely showing us where to tweak our thoughts and feelings so we can create what we desire.

I've done the above in my past stories with health. I was in very poor health for a long time in my late teens and early twenties. Health was undoubtedly my biggest wall. My story was, "If I could be healthy, I could do all the things I want to do." In that way, health became a god I served and was enslaved by. It wasn't until I surrendered to fact that I'd put all my energy into fighting, struggling and healing my body, that I realized I had to take back my life and take back my energy.

True abundance is the ability to stand still in the midst of any storm, as well as any calm. It is the ability to be the peace. It is the ability to say, "I am that I am. I am the energy behind it all." When we can go back to the point of the observer, in that space, there is always enough. In that place, there is divine and perfect health and wealth, ready to make itself known in your world in new and wonderful ways.

MEDITATION

I am now ready to let go of my feelings of lack. I'm ready to loosen my grip on trying to make things happen for myself and let abundance of all forms flow to me.

I trust that I am supported in all things and I fortify that trust everyday by letting go of outcomes and control.

I release what I "want." I am ready to fall in love with "what is."

I am filled with peace and knowing. I am whole and complete.

True abundance fills me every minute of every day whether I recognize it or not.

I am and open vessel ready to be filled with love, prosperity, and adventure

I am open to creating something new.

It is flowing. It is present. It is me.

I AM the abundant flow of all things.

I AM Abundance.

CHAPTER 27

IN SYNC

Have you ever had that experience where you happen to mention a person or think of that old friend whom you haven't seen in years then BAM! The phone rings and it's your old friend? Or you learn a new word and for the next week, you hear everyone using that word over and over again? This is synchronicity.

As the story goes, the analytical psychologist Carl Jung was working with a patient who was plagued with strange dreams about her childhood and seemed to have a block in her therapy. She would recount stories about living in Egypt but just couldn't zero in on the source of her emotional pain. One night she dreamt of a golden beetle. The next day in therapy as she described the bug and all of her pent-up angst flooded out of her. The lock on her life opened and the key was her dream about the beetle. It held significance for her as a symbol of death and rebirth in ancient Egypt and had been the final piece in solving her "neurosis."

As Jung and the patient were reveling in the breakthrough, something caught Jung's attention. Out of the corner of his eye, he saw movement on the window. Jung looked at the glass, and there was a golden beetle.

Now Jung had never seen a beetle on his window before, and while they are sometimes spotted in London, it was a highly unusual sighting, especially for that time of year. Jung, understandably shaken, realized this could be explained scientifically as mere coincidence, but it was a coincidence with profound meaning for his patient. He called it synchronicity: a "causal connecting principle or pattern of connection that cannot be explained by conventional, efficient causality." It sent a chill down his spine, and he devoted a whole book to the issue and lectured on it for many years.

We love to hear those stories. They are almost like ghost stories. Tales of the strange, unknown and unknowable. We even experience them from time to time. We sense it is when we are in the presence of universal timing. For many, this is a story about the discovery of a spooky, once in a lifetime unexplained phenomenon but actually, Jung pointed out the unfolding energy that continually surrounds us.

For most, the retelling of Jung's story would have some beckoning, "How do you explain that?" while someone else hums The Twilight Zone theme, thrilled with the unknown question of it. Jung himself labeled the event as "acausal" meaning he thought its importance was the complete lack of a cause for the effect.

Jung was an eyewitness to a cause and effect relationship. It was the energy of the universe synchronizing with a person that removed the blocks from her heart. By opening herself up to the universe, it responded with a physical gesture in return. Cause and effect.

It is funny that Jung has received all the credit in this story.

He was merely the bystander to a nameless patient able to get past her pain and suffering to achieve interdimensional alignment with the universe.

We are all capable of this power. The brain usually deals with the physical world. It translates the energies around us into something we can consciously understand. It slows down the process. It takes the energy, analyzes it and translates it into mental energy, physical energy and thought. However, in doing so there is often feedback.

Think of it as an amplifier of an electric guitar. The amp changes the electrical energy into sound energy and sends it out to the audience. The by-product is the screeching, ear-splitting feedback. When we try and absorb the energy of the universe through our brains, we get feedback in the form of worries, fret and doubts. We get into a feedback loop of painful and unwanted emotions as well. When we sync ourselves with the energy, absorb the sound through our hearts, and bypass all the feedback, what we get is beautiful music.

Others might not see the cause and effect occurring, but by opening our heart space, extraordinary things happen. When we are ready and allow ourselves to accept that we need a new job, or love, or even an extra dollar for bus fare, the universe aligns and it makes its way to us.

The universe has some amazingly sharp ears. It can hear everything – even the feedback crackling in your brain. We may think "I want to lose weight" or "I need to make more money" but wanting, needing, and thinking are not accepting. In fact, it may send out the message to the universe that you aren't prepared to do those things. Have you ever said, "I think I'll start eating healthier tomorrow," then BAM! The phone rings and your friends are inviting you to your favorite buffet restaurant.

The universe is listening to you, but are YOU listening to you?

MEDITATION

Today, I choose to be aware of my thoughts and not judge them. I am going to allow myself a free pass to simply observe all of the spaces I may be contradicting myself, where I may be wanting to have money, instead of having it, where I may be wanting a relationship but not quite ready for it.

As I observe my thoughts, I know that I am the one who can easily and effortlessly redirect them through allowing me to feel a new feeling. Today, I choose to see myself in new ways, and let go of the old stories which do not serve me in creating what I truly desire.

CHAPTER 28

TIME

O ne of Einstein's most famous breakthroughs was when he discovered that time was not a constant.

Yet, we always think of time as being one of the few things we can count on in life, as it's the same for everyone. A minute is a minute is a minute. Einstein realized that time was different depending on how fast you were moving. When he said, "Time is relative," it was hard for people to wrap their heads around it. When reporters asked him to elaborate, Einstein replied: "An hour sitting with a pretty girl on a park bench passes like a minute, but a minute sitting on a hot stove seems like an hour."

It's true, isn't it? The smartest man in the world, with his equations and mathematics, basically *proved* how we all feel. Have you ever wished there was more time in the day to get work done? Have you experienced that compressed rush during the holidays which makes them feel like they come and go too quickly? Conversely, have you ever waited to see the doctor in an emergency room? All of a sudden, time stands still. A minute is NOT a minute when you are in pain or under the gun.

Time is an illusion. We waste so much mental energy thinking about the past and the future. We regret things we've done and spend time worrying about what will be. The only true time we have is the present. Right this second is the catalyst for all future seconds to come. The light of cellular energy is always flickering. It's continually moving forward and phasing into a new plane. From one second to the next, we are always moving into a new moment of now.

We think of the past as a trail we have left behind. We let it define who we are, or direct who we will become. The truth is, in every single second, we are a new person. Every past second is a past life. Before you picked up this book, you were a different you from whom you are right now.

And right now.

And right now.

And right now.

Science has shown us that every few years, our entire body regenerates itself. Every few seconds, there are proteins in our blood which break down and regenerate on a cellular level. Those cells are made up of molecules that are always moving and always renewing. Those molecules are made up of energy which is constantly in motion, ever-changing. We are literally in a constant state of transition.

Think of it in terms of a movie. If you could slow down a movie, you would see that the reel is made up of several pictures that are only slightly different from one another, all running past our eyes so quickly, that we begin to see them as being continuous. Within our own bodies, we can direct the motion picture of us. We can literally change the movie we are in.

Sometimes, we get stuck in the same scene of our film. We recreate the same pictures over and over again. We get so used to seeing the film that we begin to identify as the story. We look back at all the memories of the film and we see those memories as our own unique history. Who we were, seems to help us form a sense of who we are – our stories help us form our identity. Loop after loop, we watch, and we create a sense of self. This is our ego. It is our individuated presence. And sometimes, this part of us isn't comfortable with adding or deleting any new pictures. It has become accustomed to the film, as is. So naturally, when we begin to change our reel – maybe add some color or special effects – the ego feels threatened. It resists, because these changes will completely change the flow of the stories. They interrupt the story arch.

So we don't change.

How many times have you been shocked that a year has gone by and you haven't started on those new years' resolutions yet, or gotten your taxes together, or looked for a new job?

One of the biggest culprits of time manipulation is resistance. We resist paying taxes, or finding a new job, or leaving a dysfunctional relationship, because we think it will be difficult and we may not have enough energy to create everything we want. For example, when we look at the reality of "I desire a new job," we also feel all of our associated stories about what jobs are, how we create them, how much energy they steal, etc. So we go into "I don't want to feel this way," and we avoid. We resist.

This sends a very mixed message to the universe, "I want this, but ewwww."

Through Universal Law of Attraction, we automatically try to steer clear of things which don't feel good, yet in this instance, the ego is co-opting your creative ability by saying, "don't look at reality. Avoid it, because it does not feel good and you don't want to keep creating more of that, do you?"

In truth, if you ever desire to change the story, you have to start right now. Acceptance is the vibrational opposite of resistance. It literally cancels out that energy – and remember, what you resist will persist. So, by moving into acceptance of where you are right now, even if you don't like it, you gift yourself the power of change.

It might be debt or a tumultuous relationship or being over-weight. We want these things to improve, but they're just too over-whelming to face. We don't like where we are, but we are afraid to initiate a move for fear it will only make things worse.

But our fears are for nothing, because every second is a new moment, and in each new moment we have the power to choose anew. By being honest and accepting (forgiving) with ourselves about what is, we create a space where we are no longer in the clutches of resistance. When you hear yourself say, "If I'm honest with myself and I am in debt and I've failed. I am a failure and I will keep creating debt, so I must deny the debt to overcome it," you're hearing that voice from a fearful, stuck space.

Do you want to stay stuck, or are you ready to realize that this form of thinking has gotten you here, and you are now ready to create something new – something abundantly different?

Find the space in your heart which says, "I've made choices in the past and those choices might not have worked out, but I have learned from them. They brought me to this moment, wherein I found this book, or this path, and I am here now, ready to make choices in alignment with who I say I am, and who I know I am, deep in my heart". If we ask and are honest with ourselves, we can remove judgment and trauma associated with where we are. We can forgive ourselves. We can stop being trapped in the past and start over in the now.

Just as we get trapped in the past, we also get mired in the future, as well. We get caught up in "what could happen" and start losing focus on what is going on right now. We start obsessing about worst-case scenarios or how sweet and perfect our life will be at source. It's a bit like driving a car and looking 100 yards ahead at all times. What about the car right in front of you? You may be so focused on the wreck ahead, that you miss the chance to take an access road or you may even hit the car ahead of you.

There is a part of us that will always want to skip ahead into the future. We want to escape the present. Especially if we aren't happy where we are right now. We want that montage scene in the movies where Rocky does all the hard training for weeks and skips ahead to being in great shape for the fight, without actually experiencing the montage, itself.

It's akin to jumping out of the womb, wanting to run. We know we have the potential, and we just want to run! Just because we can't quite figure out our muscles and legs, do we give up and never reach our goal, or do we learn to balance, walk, and then run?

This montage, walking phase, can also seem to stall time to a crawl. We start to measure ourselves against other people. They all seem to have jumped ahead of us and are already to the next level, while we are stuck down on the ground. The thing is, we haven't been watching them go up the same ladder we have one rung at a time. We get so focused on our own rung that it looks like they jumped right ahead of us.

There is an old saying, "It takes a long time for something to happen all of a sudden." A train going 100 mph doesn't stop on a dime, but it does stop. Even when it's something personal like getting in touch with yourself, you may have leaps, jumps and fast growth, yet you will still unfold over time.

People often ask me ask how to get that "cosmic light bulb moment," where everything just clicks into place and a choir of angels breaks into song. They want a life-size version of an easy button that they can push and, magically, everything falls into place. The irony is, you are that easy button. And, it happens bit by bit, until suddenly, there you are.

It is a collection of moments that lead you to the light bulb. We sometimes get stuck in one moment, where we press and press and press, doing the same things over and over and wonder why our reality doesn't change. This is the ego tapping its foot and looking at its watch, "Come on creation; get here!" And the thing is, your creation will arrive when you vibrationally align with it.

Think of it this way: If I asked you to bake me some cookies using a list of ingredients and you just threw them all in a bowl together and expected them to be finished, you are going to get some gross, mushy cookies. The cookies take time to bake. Just like the cookies, the ingredients of your life are formed from different subjects: money, love, self-worth, etc. Some of your ingredients may be perfect and readily available, while others may not have arrived yet. But when it all comes together, you will hear the timer ding and the light bulb will go off…and it will all be worth it.

When we move into harmony with all we have created, with ourselves, with love and joy, we find ourselves in the frequency of pure creation and inspiration. It's the space where the 3D universe unfolds its energy and creates a space of synchronicity. You will find you've been sitting at your desk working for an hour and have gotten three days of work done. It's the space where you catch up with an old friend on the phone and it feels like minutes, but actually hours have passed. These are the places where inspiration can slow down or speed up time.

Don't measure time with your ego but with your heart. Every second is a new you and a new beginning, and you are the ingredients and the cookie, the oven, the timer, and the baker. Make your time count, by choosing to enjoy what you do, remembering that what you do is a choice – even if that choice is simply to put a roof over your head, can you start to shift your vibration by being thankful for the choices you have made? Those choices have brought you here, to this moment, to this time, and in this time, you have the power to create anew.

MEDITATION

I choose to allow myself to unfold. Just as a baker would bake cookies, or a chef would prepare soup, I choose to become consciously aware of what ingredients I place into my life. I choose to allow myself the space and time in which to create and align with all I desire.

CHAPTER 29

BACK TO THE FUTURE

O ne of my all-time favorite movies is *"Back to the Future."* Young Marty McFly is friends with Doc Brown, essentially an absent-minded professor, who invents a device known as the "Flux Capacitor," which transforms energy and allows him to travel back in time. Marty accidentally makes changes to the past, which means his mother and father never fall in love, and he is never born. But by overcoming a series of obstacles, Marty introduces them, they fall in love and his existence is assured. In fact, by making a few changes, he returns *back to the future* to find his own circumstances have even been improved as well – all set to the music of Huey Lewis and the News's, "The Power of Love."

I love this movie so much that I even have a piece of the clock tower building set. It's a movie I could watch again and again... and in fact, I do. It's no surprise that the film was playing while I fell asleep a little while ago. The soundtrack and lines of dialogue being absorbed by my subconscious for what may have been the one-hundredth time set the stage for one of my most unusual meditation experiences ever.

What I experienced can best be described as "hypnagogia," the temporary state between consciousness and sleep, often referred to as "lucid dreaming." It allows you all the realism of the dream world but at the same time complete conscious control over your actions and with the awareness that you're still in the energies of your mind and not the physical world. It's rare to "wake up" in this state and even rarer to maintain it once you have the awareness.

Well, I experienced a very enlightening hypnagogic event.

As I fell asleep to Marty McFly, I slowly slipped into what felt like sleep, but I was most definitely awake. I was experiencing something between dreaming and meditative consciousness. I was feeling very grounded and integrated, while engrossed in the journey I was watching unfold before my eyes.

Listening to *Back to The Future* was like constructing a set in the back of my mind for my own narrative to play out. Instead of a Universal Studios sound set for Marty McFly, it was setting the stage for me to go back and replay my own history.

I was in my body, but I was waking up the house I was raised in. I knew everything I know now, but I was very much the kid I was back then. I was looking around, taking in my surroundings and feeling what it was like to be that child again, to be my adult self-observing the younger me back in time.

The series of images opened a door for me to examine all the things that occurred in my life and all the possibilities and potentials of how those experiences unfolded for me and how they influenced what I was manifesting in my present. I examined the challenges that unfolded in that past space and time and found myself enjoying seeing how they helped make me the man and the creation I became. As I remembered back to harder times in my younger days and wondered if I had handled those choices in another way how my life would be different today?

By the time I came back into my body entirely, a few hours had passed. My mouth was dry, and I was loopy and dazed. I felt like I was coming out of anesthesia after surgery. Still woozy from the experience, I shucked off the urge to go back to sleep and dove in to the rather meaningful encounter which had just taken place.

One of the messages I respond to so strongly in *Back to the Future* is that Marty is very much responsible for his own creation. He sets in motion energies in the past that affect him in the present (or his parent's future). He literally creates himself. This is something that we can all do naturally. A flux capacitor is an excellent metaphor for that part of our brains/hearts/minds that can already transform the energy of our creation. We don't need to go back in time because, as Einstein stated, time doesn't really exist. It is all relative – meaning, to an extent, we choose our current roles based on our perceptions of the past; the past itself does not really exist. It is all one stream of consciousness, and we have the power to change our responses, and thus, like Marty, change the relationship to both the past and the present.

We are made of energy that doesn't know age or time the way we cling to it in the physical representation of our reality. We have been, will be, and always are the energy that is continually creating who we are.

Too often people wish they could travel in time because they lament their past decisions or think that their life needs to be "corrected" to have the perfect outcome. They bemoan, "If only I could go back and change things!" or "If only I could have a do-over."

The two most hopelessly overused words in the world: "If only."

There is no need to change the circumstances of the past if you can transform the energy it created. Seeing it from an Observer perspective allows you to change the past by realizing that all those perceived failures and face plants were and are brilliant and dramatic brush strokes on the painting that is your life. They brought you to this moment right now, and this moment right now is the moment in which you have the power to create all other experiences.

Realizing the beauty of your past, the good, the bad, and the ugly and accepting all of it is the key to moving forward and creating your future – not wanting to change the physical situation but learn from it and appreciating the self-creating energies that took place. There is much to be gained by transforming the energy you receive from past embarrassments or unfortunate events, so they aren't "mistakes" that make you cringe but "Eureka!" moments that teach you great lessons.

Doc Brown's flux capacitor merely changed speed energy into time travel energy. Your flux capacitor has the power to transform what was once a regret to what is now a maybe a lesson, an opportunity to choose a new door, or just one of multiple pieces that allow you to embody the power of love.

MEDITATION

I am my own creation.

Nothing in the past needs to be corrected or resolved.

My mistakes are not tragedies. They help shape my experience and inform my life.

Each day brings a new opportunity to grow, love, shape your life's creation.

All I have ever been has led me to this moment of now, a moment where I realize at a deep level, I hold the Power and the Love, to choose anew.

CHAPTER 30

RELATIONSHIPS

If I gave you a magical golden pen and told you that anything you wrote would come to pass, how would the story you write change your life?

It's no surprise in the complex world in which we live that some of us have debilitating blocks around relationships. We're afraid if we put ourselves out there, panic will ensue because we have absolutely no clue as to what the future will bring. We think to ourselves, "I can't do this. I have no idea what will happen or how I'll be able to handle it." While we may deeply desire a loving relationship, we find ourselves terrified of what lies ahead. We believe we'll mess everything up and add to the hurt and discord already in our life (or in others) and we plead to ourselves, "I've failed before, and I cannot go through it again. I don't want to be vulnerable. I don't want the pain."

We desperately want to try again, but deep down we feel unwor-

177

thy of a relationship and petrified we won't be received and loved the way we need to be.

But what if I told you there was a button in your mind and that pushing that button allowed you to pause every single story you've ever imagined, created, or thought into existence? What if you had the freedom to choose a new beginning, a new experience, a new vision of relationships and love?

Sometimes, we want out of relationships because we feel stuck and unable to choose our path going forward. We struggle with this in our relationship with ourselves as well. We don't like who we are, where we are, or what were' doing because we feel we don't have choices anymore. We feel we've been shoved into a situation, even if it's through decisions we ourselves have made. We don't' like them, so we go into revolt mode, and energetically wave our middle fingers in the air like we just don't care.

But actually, we do care. We care very deeply.

We want to be free to choose our life, but there are limiting beliefs around what freedom means and who'll get hurt if we free ourselves. So many times we make a choice and think we have to stay there and make it work or suffer with it, but there is nothing to be gained by imprisoning yourself and closing the door to the love you so richly deserve.

Always remember, you chose once, and you are free to choose again. If you have permission to choose again, you begin to choose your way into something that feels right for you. Your life begins to shift, and you open up more and more and more to those things that feel better, that feel restorative and transformational.

The issue is not about leaving a partner, a job or a space. It's about feeling so free to choose you completely change your perception. You're now able to find gifts in that space and remember why you chose that journey in the first place.

Remember the button in your mind? Well, pressing that button stops all the old stories. As they stop, love washes away all those stories to heal any wounds from those stories and to create wholeness. From this space, we now become realized in a new way. We can *feel* our ideal relationship.

Divine love is that button and you don't have to do or be anything to feel that love. You are that love – even if you have forgotten it. All you have to do to press that button is tune in to what pure, divine source energy feels like, free of all stories, infinitely freeing, nourishing, and loving.

Your stories are just that- stories. Stories you have told yourself. Stories that were thrust upon you by others. As you begin to change your stories, other people begin to change. They begin to play the roles you write for them in your energy field.

You have the power to create your world, not just through your thoughts, but through your unconscious expectations, and you change those expectations by changing how you feel. You have the ability to experience relationships that create more wholeness in you, more wellness, more love, more peace, more vibrancy, more joy. You have everything you need to move into the creation of all you desire, you just have to choose anew.

Begin by allowing yourself to feel. Turn off the mind; release the stories of who you are and who you've been so you can create the story of who you are to become.

You're ready to move beyond the stories and the limitations, the frustration, and move into a place of absolute love and trust. Release the bonds of karma; release the *belief* in karma, release karma itself. Cut the cords, chains, and servitude and declare,

"I am self-love."

Feel into what that would mean. What would it feel like if there were no block to loving all you are? What if you allowed yourself to make choices in alignment with an open heart? How might your world change? If lack or limitation spring to mind, consciously choose again. Move back into the heart space and choose to feel a divine, protective, joyful, nurturing, supportive love. Even if you've never felt that before, what might it feel like?

It's time to feel what it feels like to truly know that you are self-love. If you truly know it, you are it. You are self-love.

Many years ago, I wrote what I often refer to as the prayer of empowerment. Prayer for me, means knowing. I remember a story from my childhood about three people of different faiths who were all called to pray over a dry, dead field of crops. As the three journeyed into the field, they all began to pray. A few moments later, the first of the three walked back to the car. About an hour later, the other two joined, and asked, "Why didn't you pray longer?"

The response is something I have remembered for a very long time. "Prayer for me is not about asking, or begging. It is not about whether I deserve it or whether someone else deserves it or not. It is about knowing it as complete, and feeling thankful in the whole-ness. I walked out and smelled the rain. I felt what it would feel like for my toes to be wet and squishy in the soil. I knew in my being it was so, and I gave thanks that it was."

With that energy, I wrote this prayer: "I allow all energy to support me. I let down my walls and my guard. I invite myself to come out and play in the world where I am safe and cherished and celebrated and loved. I allow and direct all energy to honor and bless me. I direct and allow all energy to celebrate and bless me. I direct and allow all energy to love me."

Feel that as your truth and energy, the truth and energy of love in action.

The energy of love is like a piece of paper upon which you've written everything your heart desires. By boldly declaring your true desires, you are mailing that letter to the Universe. It's taking that piece of paper, turning it into programming, then feeding it into the hologram of you. You're plugging the new coordinates into your energy system saying, "This is what I'm choosing to construct. This is the world I'm choosing to create. I'm authoring a new program." Begin to feel what it's like to be in a new place, to be loved, celebrated and honored not only by yourself, but by everyone around you.

You're a miracle just by being here. You are alive. You are amazing. You are a beautiful child of God. You contain every single piece of this beautiful universe within the smallest cell of you. This world would not exist without you. Feel the power of that statement and invite the universe to mirror that love right back to you with every single step you take.

Feel what it would feel like to be completely loved, shared, respected, and honored, to feel safe and warm and loved.

Feel what it would feel like to receive that from others, and to feel it from self.

The wholeness that you commit to is you being the whole unto yourself. The wholeness of you is ever expansive and as you become more whole and happy, more wholeness and happiness is compounded in you.

Feel what it would feel like in your sense of wholeness, joy, completion and love to be met by a partner of equal wholeness, joy, completion, and love.

Feel what it would feel like to grow with that person, those people. Feel what it would feel like to be a part of something. To be cherished and loved as part of the whole that you are.

You and you alone write your story of love. You bring into existence, into physical reality, into experience, into physical manifestation this love, this being-ness, this joy, this peace, this radiance, and this celebration.

Feel what it feels like to be held, loved, and allow you to give of yourself and to be received freely in truth and beauty, harmony and love.

Feel what it feels like to be truly seen one hundred percent and not have to hide one single thing about who you are, what your dreams are, or what you want.

Feel what it feels like to have someone take your hand and hold it in theirs and look deep into your eyes, and say, "I see you, and I love you. I see you and I love you. And I see you seeing me, and I see you loving me."

This is what it feels like to know you are divine love.

This is what it feels like to know you are self-love.

This is what it feels like to be held safe in love.

Know that this energy is you. You have access to this energy twenty-four hours a day. You are loved by yourself and by the universe.

You are celebrated.

Give yourself permission to love yourself, even when you see others not loving themselves. Shine your light, and that light attracts to you the light of others. Together you and the light of your beloved light up the world. In lighting up your world, you light up the entire world. This is what you deserve. It's who you are. It's what you now have.

You are open to the experience of love.

MEDITATION

I am the creation of me, my world, my universe, my body, and my thoughts.

I am the direction of the frequency of all energy, and I am directing that all energy be harmoniously balanced in the moment of now.

I am whole I am that I am I accept that I am the creation of all creation.

I am powerful, and I understand that I am a being worthy of love and nurturing as well as giving love and nurturing.

My expression of love is not reserved for partners or romantic relationships alone. It's for co-workers, family, friends, business partners, beloved pets and total strangers.

I write my own story.

I create my life now as the direction of my light.

I am the direction of that light.

I am the creation of that light.

I am allowing that light to come forward and shine in me, now and forever.

EPILOGUE

Every day, significant events are unfolding in the world, and inside of you. Key issues are being brought to the surface and brought to the light. They are being exposed in a space and place where there have been patterns, emotions or vibrations calling out for something new. As we shift energetically into a new space, the old ways quickly become outmoded, outdated, and unsupported on the planet. So, we get to choose if we would like to realign and move into a new space – a space where we open the heart and create from love, freedom, and plenty.

In terms of consciousness and how far we have come – and will continue to go – think about what was permissible a hundred years ago. Who could vote and who couldn't vote, who counted as a person and who didn't count as a person. Now look back several hundreds of years. Imagine what was available for us to do in our lives, how to live our lives, careers that we could choose, and spiritual paths we could take. There were certain ideas and concepts that could not even be translated into a spoken language. You would have to rely on someone else's interpretation and experience of the divine and see the world through their eyes.

We are now stepping into a new collective space of choice.

The balance of old and the new are now meeting in the middle. Some are creating breathtaking spaces of love and joy. Others are coming together like two flints creating a spark and igniting a fire- a fire that is there to release into the light all things that need to be seen and shared and shown in our lives – the things that make our extraordinary lives worth living.

No matter what happens in life, always remember that you are the chooser and the choice. When you can create from your space of centered, divine love, there is nothing you cannot accomplish, nothing you cannot be.

You are love, expressing itself in action, and you are amazing.

When you forget, go back and read this book. Feel into the meditations at the ends of each chapter, and make the choice to remember "I am divine love." Feel what that feels like. Let yourself absorb it more and more, until you fully become it, that there may be love in all your being. That love will radiate from your being, and you will experience what it is to truly be a miracle in the making, and a miracle made manifest, in every moment of life's great adventure.

ACKNOWLEDGEMENTS

First and foremost, I want to thank my friends, my family, my amazing team, and every person who reads a copy of this book. This is for you. Your energy, your questions, your love, your support, and your journey have all had a hand in creating this book.

Thank you to David Hancock, my publisher and friend, for believing in this book, for seeing my vision and helping expand upon it. Sincere thanks to Bonnie Rauch and everyone at Morgan James Publishing.

Many thanks to Darius Barazandeh, Jan Carpenter, Sonya Darian, Debe Fennell, David Ratner, Mike Mejer, Jennifer McLean, Mike Pearson and Mariah Corell for giving me such love and support over the years.

To Mairead McAllister, thank you! Your support, love, and energy, have been a never ending catalyst for growth.

ABOUT THE AUTHOR

J arrad Hewett is a 3 Time Best-Selling Author, Multi- Dimensional Energy Expert, and Founder of the Quantum Technology Frequency Method™ He is the Best-Selling Author of *Love, Life, God: The Journey of Creation* as well as the co-author of the International #1 Best-Selling *The Big E – Everything is Energy: Unleashing The Power of Everyday Wisdom*. His most recent book, *The Gospel of You: The Truth About God, Religion, and Who You Really Are* is available now. Jarrad's in-depth energy work has led to 3 #1 Best-Selling books, a devoted client list featuring some of the biggest and most well-known names in the Self Help and Spiritual Movements, as well as numerous radio & television show appearances – he can also be heard on CMT, HGTV, DIY, and the Disney Channel.

Morgan James makes all of our titles available
through the Library for All Charity Organization.

www.LibraryForAll.org

CPSIA information can be obtained
at www.ICGtesting.com
Printed in the USA
LVHW032029150119
604026LV00001B/1/P